Routledge Revivals

Dynamic Investment Planning

In dynamic investment planning the time of investment is a significant issue. By simplifying the mathematical notation, the author of this book seeks to make control theory a practical tool that can be applied to the problem of timing.

The book, first published in 1977, begins with an introduction to one important approach to control theory – dynamic programming. Then some of the relevant literature that deals with investment decision-making is reviewed. This is followed by a mathematically formulated planning model. The computational aspects of the model are discussed and a complete computer flow chart is given.

The second part of the book gives a thorough application of the theory by means of a detailed case study – the planning of a steel industry. The case study illustrates how a fairly abstract dynamic analysis can be effectively integrated with practical decision-making concerns.

This book is ideal for students of economics and business.

Dynamic Investment Planning

M. H. I. Dore

Routledge
Taylor & Francis Group

First published in 1977
by Croom Helm Ltd

This edition first published in 2015 by Routledge
2 Park Square, Milton Park, Abingdon, Oxon, OX14 4RN
and by Routledge
711 Third Avenue, New York, NY 10017

Routledge is an imprint of the Taylor & Francis Group, an informa business

Publisher's Note
The publisher has gone to great lengths to ensure the quality of this
reprint but points out that some imperfections in the original copies may
be apparent.

Disclaimer
The publisher has made every effort to trace copyright holders and
welcomes correspondence from those they have been unable to contact.

A Library of Congress record exists under LC control number: 77371590

ISBN 13: 978-1-138-83984-7 (hbk)
ISBN 13: 978-1-315-73320-3 (ebk)

DYNAMIC INVESTMENT PLANNING

M.H.I. DORE

CROOM HELM   LONDON

© 1977 M.H.I. Dore
Croom Helm Ltd,
2-10 St John's Road, London SW11

British Library Cataloguing in Publication Data

Dore, M H I
    Dynamic investment planning.
    1. Capital investments – Mathematical models
    2. Dynamic programming
    I. Title
    658.1'527   HG4028.C4

    ISBN 0-85664-415-3

Printed in Great Britain by offset lithography by
Billing & Sons Ltd, Guildford, London and Worcester

CONTENTS

Preface

PREFACE

The application of modern control theory to economics began with the seminal article by Frank Ramsey in 1928. After a renewed interest in the subject matter, a great deal of work has appeared which is collectively referred to as 'optimum growth theory'. Most of this work has been (appropriately) concerned with important theoretical issues of a macroeconomic nature such as aggregate savings.

It is my belief that the theoretical frontiers have perhaps been pursued far enough to begin some tentative applied work so that optimum growth type analysis may become one more tool in the applied economist's tool kit. This book, I hope, is one such modest attempt. It is an application of control theory to the problem of dynamic investment planning, i.e., where the timing of investment is a significant issue. The application is confined to a single industry and it assumes that there is no interaction between the chosen industry and the rest of the economy. The assumption is of course patently untrue. Economic theory can certainly handle many kinds of interactions and, in a dynamic context, these interactions can be so overwhelming that any optimal policy obtained from an optimisation exercise would pall into insignificance.

I acknowledge my guilt in ignoring these interactions but, in mitigation, would say that a large task, such as an economy-wide optimum growth plan, would probably require a team of researchers with many an insight into theoretical considerations too complex for me.

I have a more limited aim in mind. Modern contron theory is not all that difficult if one can simplify the obfuscating notation. The key ideas can be made intuitively appealing, or rather they have already been made so. It is then a small step to show to the practical decision-maker how the theory can be mobilised for better economic decisions when the payoffs for the right decisions are high.

The book is based on a doctoral dissertation completed in 1975 at Nuffield College, Oxford. While there I had the privilege of receiving help and advice from a number of dons at Nuffield. My first debt is to Jim Mirrlees who helped me to sharpen the analysis on a number of points. I also learnt from him that while it is always necessary to make assumptions in economics, intellectual optimality requires that one minimises the set of assumptions. I have also benefitted from comments made by Allen Brown, Alan Gelb, Francis Seton and Nick Stern who all read large parts of early drafts of the doctoral dissertation.

Clive Payne of Nuffield College provided expert computational help besides writing the computer codes for me and I am greatly indebted to him.

Coffee time at Nuffield I often selfishly used as free tutorials, as one often can, and I benefitted from talking to other Nuffield economists. Aubrey Silberston was particularly helpful in arranging access to published data on steel technology, and the British Steel Corporation heartily cooperated.

I hasten to add that I alone am responsible for any remaining deficiencies in this work.

My wife shared with me the trying experience of doing research and enabled me to persevere. I don't think I would have liked to have done it without her.

October 1976.   M.H.I. Dore

PART ONE: THEORY

1 INTRODUCTION

1.1 Investment and 'Dynamics'

In an economic sense all investment is a withdrawal from present day consumption to augment future consumption in the aggregate. This applies to the individual, to the firm as well as to the public authority. The individual *invests* in a car[1] because he values the facilities the car will provide him over a period more than the satisfaction he would have derived by spending the money in some other way. Similarly a firm makes a particular investment because its managers think that that particular investment augments future profits, which will be distributed to its shareholders, and possibly consumed.

However the aggregate additional future consumption possibility is usually made available over a period of time. An immediate problem is how to value the net additions to possible consumption when they are spread out over time. In the case of the individual who buys a car, it is safe to assume he knows. In the case of the firm, or the individual acting as a firm, and the public authority, the presumption of knowledge will not do: the firm or the public authority will often want to justify its investment decision.

The most common and consistent criterion used to make the consumption benefits in different time periods comparable is known as the present value method. The standard approach then is to consider mutually exclusive projects by comparing the total net benefits in present value terms and accepting the project with the highest net present value (NPV).

Is this static criterion an adequate guide for investment decisions for firms and public authorities? The answer is that in some cases it may be adequate, but in the case of large investments the decision-maker will want to be sure he had not overlooked any other relevant aspect of the decision problem. For example, is the size of NPV sensitive to the *time segment* over which the project will operate? But if this aspect is admitted as relevant then all other competing investment projects that were rejected may have to be screened anew.

It is a central hypothesis of this book that the static criterion of investment decisions can be misleading when for many projects it is obvious that the timing of the project should be included as a 'choice variable'. The inadequacy of the criterion is due in part to the nature of investment, and to the nature of time itself.

Much has been written about the nature of investment and this need not delay us here. For example, economists accept that most major investments have 'political' consequences in so far as the investment affects inter-generational distribution of income; that being irreversible every investment alters the options open to future generations, and so on.

The nature of time is less explicitly considered if ever. It sounds banal to state that not only is time a sequence of time periods but that it is a particular sequence, which is of course irreversible. This, it is maintained here, has a profound consequence on decision-making. Whenever a decision-problem is defined over say a five or twenty year period, the time segment involved is always a particular segment, not just any time segment. This characteristic of time is almost invariably lost when one begins to speak of a 'planning horizon', and should be borne in mind.

When time is treated in the above sense in a decision-problem, then the latter is dynamic, and time becomes a legitimate choice variable in the decision-problem. (Throughout this book 'dynamic' must be understood in this technical sense.)

1.2 Appropriate Tools

A dynamic decision-problem is of course synonymous with a dynamic optimisation problem, since the objective is to arrive at an optimal decision. The text books give three mathematical methods, all intimately related, that are oriented towards solving such problems. The historically oldest method, the calculus of variations is suitable only for a limited kind of dynamic optimisation problem. Next came Richard Bellman's method of Dynamic Programming, developed in the 1950s, which subsumes all the necessary conditions for an optimum given by the calculus of variations (Bellman and Dreyfus [4]). Finally in 1962 Pontryagin and his associates (see Pontryagin *et al.* [29]) published what may be regarded as a dynamic generalisation of the method of Lagrange. Both methods are collectively known as modern *control theory*, and are widely used in the engineering sciences.

In this book the dynamic programming method is used as it turns out to be suitable for the special characteristics of the dynamic investment problem. A leisurely introduction to dynamic programming will be found in Chapter 2, which may be omitted by those already familiar with the technique.

1.3 Capturing the Characteristics of the Problem

Empirical research shows that most manufacturing industries, and all
process industries (i.e., aluminium, steel, petro-chemicals, etc.) exhibit
economies of scale both in investment and in operating costs. Secondly
with burgeoning technological progress investment in industry has
become 'lumpy'. This lumpiness has two dimensions: the initial lump
for a minimum plant size is very large, and subsequently larger plant
sizes are discrete, due to technical and physical constraints. However
not all technically balanced and feasible plant sizes beyond the
minimum plant size are of economic interest. Thus the determinants of
lumpiness are both technological as well as economic. If an investment
planning model is to be realistic then it must reflect these characteristics
of industrial plants.

The dynamic optimisation model that includes the above features
must of course have an *objective* or *criterion function* which should be
an economic quantity and the investment options must be evaluated in
the light of this criterion. It is reasonable to assume that the criterion
should be the real *net* impact of the investment under consideration.
For most industries the output is tradeable across national boundaries
and so the impact is largely on the country's foreign trade. (Either the
output will be exported or it will replace what used to be imported, or
it may do both in parts.) The impact is then best 'added up' in terms of
some convenient numeraire such as foreign exchange.

It is clear that there is still some leeway in the precise specification
of the criterion. One approach is simply to minimise all costs associated
with the project for a given horizon; another approach is to maximise
the net benefits over the horizon. It turns out that when 'sacrifices' are
suitably defined, the minimisation of sacrifices is equivalent to the
maximisation of net benefits.

However, the economies of scale make this a 'non-convex'
optimisation problem which typically lead to extreme solutions –
unless further constrained. Since domestic demand is anyway a major
consideration it can be used to achieve this end, and if the framework
is dynamic and one of the alternatives is importing, it is possible to
obtain an optimal mix of domestic production and imports. In this way
the optimal timing as well as the scale of investment can be determined.
The analytical framework is appropriate both for private or publicly
owned industry. The latter in particular would want to incorporate
certain social goals as well into the criterion function and this can be
readily done (see Chapter 9).

The dynamic optimisation of a non-convex problem can be computed by suitably translating the problem into discrete terms and by reformulating the criterion function as a functional recurrence relation of dynamic programming. The optimal solutions are of course a function of the initial parameters, and provided these parameters are well established, the results can be operationally useful, especially if some sensitivity analysis is also carried out.

Thus the aim of this book is two-fold. The first is to present aspects of the theory of dynamic investment planning with a measure of rigour, but, one hopes, without the obfuscating notation that normally accompanies the use of modern control theory. The second aim, as the subtitle of the book suggests, is to give a thorough application of the theory by means of a case study, which is pursued to a fairly low level of abstraction, i.e., as close to real life as possible. In this way it is hoped to demonstrate the operational validity of the theory to the decision-maker.

1.4 An Overview

As stated above, the next chapter is a heuristic guide to the main ideas of dynamic programming. Chapter 3 is a brief survey of some approaches to dynamic investment planning and also introduces in an informal manner the basic model of Chapter 4, where it is rigourously expounded. It is first formulated in continuous-time and then reformulated in discrete-time, i.e., suitable for computation. Chapter 5 covers the computational aspects of the model, where the basic algorithm is explained and the reader is taken step by step through the computer flow chart which is given at the end of the chapter. This completes Part One of the book.

Part Two, devoted to application of the theory, begins with Chapter 6 which introduces the case study, viz. the planning of a steel industry, and its relevant aspects. In Chapter 7 all the required parameters are discussed and gathered together for computations, the results of which cover Chapter 8. The particular numerical results are based on Zambian data, where the question of timing and scale of investment in a steel industry was under active consideration during 1972-75. A fairly wide ranging sensitivity analysis is also presented in Chapter 8. The next chapter is an extension of the model to incorporate principles of social cost-benefit theory, and further numerical results are given. Chapter 10 brings in some doses of realism and attempts to show how a fairly abstract dynamic analysis can be effectively integrated with practical decision-making concerns. Lastly in Chapter 11 some general conclusions are noted.

Notes

1. The example is chosen to exclude "speculative investment" – a quick "killing" – which properly belongs to the realm of gambling.

2 INTRODUCTION TO DYNAMIC PROGRAMMING

The purpose of this chapter is to provide a brief and heuristic introduction to the technique of dynamic programming. The treatment given here is naturally limited and those interested can consult a number of recent introductions to the subject.[1] For the sake of simplicity *time*, which is the essence of the subject matter of this book, is not introduced here. But some remarks on the incorporation of time will be made towards the end of the chapter.

2.1 Dynamic Programming: An Example

Perhaps a defining characteristic of the technique of dynamic programming (DP) is treatment of a particular problem that requires a solution as a member of a set of problems which have the same features. An algorithm for the set or class of problems is then devised, and the solution to the original problem emerges as a special case. Thus for example, suppose the original problem is to determine whether to invest or not (and at what time period of course) when the initial production capacity for a particular commodity is zero. Then DP handles this by developing a solution for any initial capacity, and the solution of zero initial capacity is determined as a special case.

Consider the following simple example of constrained optimisation:

Maximise	$f = (4x_1 + 5x_2)$	(2.1)
subject to	$2x_1 + x_2 \leqslant 6$	(2.2)
	$x_1, x_2 \geqslant 0$	(2.3)

A number of economic interpretations of this problem are possible. One possibility is to let x_1 and x_2 be quantities of goods 1 and 2 that are produced on the same machine (say), and they take up 2 hours and 1 hour respectively for each unit produced. Total machine time available is 6 hours per day, and the two goods contribute to the firm's total profit in the ratio of 4:5. The problem is then to determine the quantities of goods 1 and 2 that must be produced in order to maximise profits.

Since (2.1)-(2.3) is a linear programming problem with two variables, a graphical solution is possible. In Fig. 2.1, x_1 and x_2 are placed respectively on the horizontal and vertical axis. The line AB reflects the constraint of total available machine time, and the ratio in which the

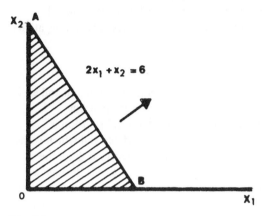

Fig. 2.1

two goods would take up the total machine time if the machine was fully utilised. The arrow gives the 'preference' direction: the more of goods 1 and 2 are produced the more the profits. But line AB prescribes the limits of the maximum amount of the goods that can be produced.

Obviously one needs to consider only points A and B, since any point or combination of the two goods inside the shaded area would not maximise profits. Inside the shaded area, the output of one good can be increased without a reduction in the output of the other and so raise profits.

It is clear that point A represents the output combination that maximises profits: 6 units of good 2 should be produced and none of good 1. Then the contribution to the firm's total profits is 30 monetary units. The optimal solution of (2.1)-(2.3) can be written as:

$$f = 30$$
$$x_1^* = 0$$
$$x_2^* = 6$$

How would the solution to (2.1)-(2.3) be tackled in the framework of DP? This will now be considered in detail in order to illustrate the essential characteristics of DP.

In general, the structure of a DP problem is made up of the following:

(a)   a set of *state* variables;

(b)   a set of *decision* or *control* variables;

(c)   a set of constraints on the state variables or the control variables, or both; typically some of these are non-negativity constraints;

(d)   an objective function.

Each decision makes a contribution to the objective function and each decision transforms the state variable(s). It is only when the transformation is mathematically tractable that a DP solution is feasible. Indeed identifying which is the state variable and which is the control variable is often half of the problem; once this is done the transformation function becomes apparent. DP proceeds through a series of 'transformations': it is convenient to dub each transformation a stage. It is for this reason that DP is often described as a method of *multi-stage optimisation*.

What then are the state variables and the decision variables in the problem (2.1)-(2.3) given above?

Since the whole object of the exercise is to determine the values of x_1 and x_2, clearly these must be the decision variables. The state variable (there is only one in this simple example), is the available machine time — both initially and at each subsequent stage. Perhaps it is clearer if one calls it 'the state of the available machine time'.

The state of the available machine time changes at each stage and is in fact dependent on the decision variables. But if the previous sentence can be formulated mathematically, it is none other than the transformation function.

Now in problem (2.1)-(2.3), it does not matter whether good 1 or good 2 is produced 'first' on the machine: the order affects neither profitability nor the constant machine times of each good. Therefore it does not matter whether good 1 or good 2 is produced first. Then the schematic diagram of Fig. 2.2 represents a convenient series of transformations. At the beginning of the first stage there is an 'input' of 6 machine hours, which after the first stage is transformed into $6 - 2x_1$ (whatever the value of x_1) and after stage 2 it is further

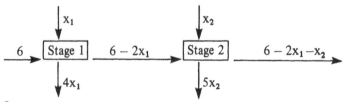

Fig. 2.2

The 'output' of stage 1 is a contribution to profits of $4x_1$ — whatever the value of x_1 — and the 'output' of stage 2 is a contribution to profits of $5x_2$ — whatever the value of x_2.

As mentioned before, the order in which the problem is solved — whether with x_1 first or with x_2 first — is immaterial here. However, with the issue of dynamic investment planning dealt with later in the book, time is a real variable and the irreversible nature of time must be captured in the solution procedure. Time then finds its natural expression in the stages and the optimisation is carried out *backwards*, i.e., stage n is optimised before stage n - 1, and stage 2 is optimised before stage 1.

In order to provide a direct parallel later, it would be interesting to solve problem (2.1)-(2.3) backwards. Consider Fig. 2.2 again. Treat the value of x_1 as a parameter, say $x_1 = \bar{x}_1$, and solve Stage 2 with respect to decision variable x_2, as follows:

$$f_1 = \max_{x_2} (5x_2) \tag{2.4}$$

subject to

$$x_2 \leqslant 6 - 2\bar{x}_1 \tag{2.5}$$
$$x_2 \geqslant 0 \tag{2.6}$$

The highest possible value of x_2 that respects (2.5) and (2.6) is when equality holds in (2.5): i.e., $x_2 = 6 - 2\bar{x}_1$. Substituting this value into (2.4) we have

$$f_1 = \max [5(6 - 2\bar{x}_1)]$$
$$= \max [30 - 10\bar{x}_1]$$

where $\bar{x}_1$ is a parameter.

Now stage 1 may be optimised with respect to x_1, treating stage 2 as if 'it had already happened' since we are going backwards:

$$f_2 = \max_{x_1} [4x_1 + f_1]$$
$$= \max_{x_1} [4x_1 + 30 - 10x_1]$$
$$= \max_{x_1} [30 - 6x_1] \tag{2.7}$$

subject to

$$2x_1 \leqslant 6 \tag{2.8}$$
$$x_1 \geqslant 0 \tag{2.9}$$

It is obvious from (2.8) and (2.9) that x_1 must lie between 0 and 3 inclusive (see Fig. 2.1 again). Maximising (2.7) with respect to x_1 yields the optimal value of $x_1 = 0$, for (2.7) is a decreasing function of x_1.

In summary form the optimal solution is:

$f_2 = 30$ (monetary units)
$x_1^* = 0$
$x_2^* = 6$ (obtained from 2.5)

The set of optimal decisions, viz. x_1^* and x_2^*, is called the *optimal policy*.

2.2 Dynamic Programming: Some Generalisations

Having solved the problem, it might be worthwhile to go back and discuss the transformation function and the objective function.

It is not difficult to see the transformation function in the series of transformations: see Fig. 2.2 again. Let us generalise the initial state of the available machine time and call it the variable y:

$$y_0 = 6 \tag{2.10}$$

Then after the first decision we have

$$y_1 = y_0 - 2x_1 \tag{2.11}$$

and after the second decision

$$y_2 = y_1 - x_2 \tag{2.12}$$

Equations (2.10)-(2.12) are in fact the transformation functions. Note that if (2.10) is now dropped, the transformation functions are valid for *any* initial state of the machine, not just when $y = 6$. This is a very simple example of embedding a particular problem, in which the initial state is 6, into a general class of problems with any possible initial state.

Thus in general form the transformation function can be written as follows: the state variable at any stage depends on the state variable at the previous stage and the decision variable of the previous stage. Adopting now the more customary notation, let x(i) be the state variable at stage 1, and let u(i) be the decision variable at stage i. Mathematically, the transformation function is:

$$x(i + 1) = g[x(i), u(i)] \quad . \tag{2.13}$$

We turn now to the objective function. It is clear from (2.7) that the two stage contributions to profits, or returns as they will be called from here onwards, were added together. This additivity is a crucial requirement of DP. Let

H(i) = return from stage i   .

Then the total return from all N stages, called J, is

$$J = \sum_{i=1}^{N} H(i) \tag{2.14}$$

Now if each H(.) depends on the initial state, x(1), and the series of decisions u(1), u(2), . . . u(N), we can write (2.14) as:

$$J = J[x(1), u(1), \ldots, u(N)] \quad . \tag{2.15}$$

As we are interested in the maximum[2] of (2.15), define a new function

$$f_N[x(1)] \equiv \max_{u(1), \ldots, u(N)} [J[x(1), u(1), \ldots u(N)]] \tag{2.16}$$

The l.h.s. of (2.16) simply defines the optimal return over N stages beginning with state x(1). Since (2.15) is a function of x(1) and N independent variables u(1), u(2), . . . , u(N), the N maximisations can be carried out in any order we like. This being the case, it is convenient to suppose that the maximisation with respect to u(1) is carried out last, so that

$$f_N[x(1)] = \max_{u(1)} \left\{ \max_{u(2), \ldots, u(N)} [J[x(1), u(1), \ldots, u(N)]] \right\} \tag{2.17}$$

Consider first the inner maximisation only in (2.17). It is independent of the return from the first stage which is H(1). This means the inner maximisation of (2.17) can be written

$$H(1) + \max_{u(2), \ldots, u(N)} [J[x(2), u(2), \ldots, u(N)]] \tag{2.18}$$

But the second term of (2.18) can be written using the definition of (2.16), for it is nothing more than the optimal return over $N - 1$ stages starting with $x(2)$, i.e. $f_{N-1}[x(2)]$. Now (2.17) can be rewritten using (2.16) and (2.18):

$$f_N[x(1)] = \max_{u(1)} [H(1) + f_{N-1}[x(2)]] \tag{2.19}$$

Equation (2.19) states that the optimal return over N stages is: the optimal return over $N - 1$ stages plus the optimal return over the first stage.

The formalism is completed if we recall the transformation function (2.13). Putting $i = 1$ into (2.13) means that (2.19) can be written in the following standard form:

$$f_N[x(1)] = \max_{u(1)} [H(1) + f_{N-1}[g[x(1), u(1)]]] . \tag{2.20}$$

Equation (2.20) is the standard *functional recurrence relation* of DP for processes that are independent of time.[3] The split-up of the l.h.s. into two terms on the r.h.s. in (2.20) implies Bellman's Principle of Optimality which is illustrated and proved in Chapter 4, p.45. In fact the derivation of the (2.20) is much simpler if the Principle of Optimality is used.

Finally, a note on backward and forward recursion is appropriate. In the algorithm illustrated in Section 2.1, backward recursion was employed. However when the order of the stages is arbitrary, as in that example, both backward and forward recursion are feasible. In that particular example all that would be required would be to reverse the direction of Fig. 2.2 and invert the transformation functions.

However, with time dependent processes, the direction is not arbitrary and backward recursion is essential. Of course with a time dependent process, equation (2.20) will have an additional argument, time. For example, the optimisation may be over N years, and each stage becomes a year.

It must be emphasised that the above is a very brief introduction to the basic approach of DP. Readers interested in acquiring a better understanding of the breadth and scope of DP may consult M. Beckman [3], Jacobs [19], and Donardo [12]. The latter is advanced but is an excellent formalisation of a large class of sequential decision processes, using concepts that would appeal to the applied economist as well as the operations research analyst.

The next chapter returns to the central issues of dynamic investment planning and contains a selective review of published work in the field.

Notes

1. See below.
2. The exposition in this chapter is confined to a maximisation problem, as it is obvious that the procedure is equally applicable to a minimisation problem.
3. Also called 'autonomous'' or 'stationary'. See Chapter 3 (p.36 and p.39 n.8) for the distinction between autonomous and non-autonomous processes.

3 DYNAMIC INVESTMENT PLANNING: A SURVEY

In this chapter we return to the problem of the timing of investment that was posed in Chapter 1. The subject matter has a history that is closely tied to that of cost-benefit analysis and welfare economics.

Of particular relevance is the work of Stephen Marglin [25], Alan Manne [23], [24], and his associates Donald Erlenkotter and T.N. Srinivasan. Section 3.1 is a brief survey[1] of their approach to the problem of dynamic investment planning. Section 3.2 contains a verbal statement of our own model, which is then compared with the approaches surveyed in Section 3.1.

3.1 Investment Timing

The earliest and most systematic treatment of the central issue of dynamic investment planning, namely the timing of investment, is given by Marglin. He shows that the usual static rule of accepting a project that has the highest positive net present value need not necessarily be dominant when the timing of construction is also a choice variable. Indeed delaying the construction time could increase the net present value, and the fact that the latter is positive at the present time is not sufficient reason to accept the project now.

More formally Marglin's analysis is as follows. Let u represent calendar time, and t the time when the project was constructed. Then (u-t) is the 'age' of the project — a concept that generalises two characteristics of projects, viz. the gestation lag at the beginning and falling output (or higher maintenance costs) towards the end of the project's life. Now assume that the benefits can be written as:

$$B(u, u\text{-}t) = P(u) \cdot X(u\text{-}t) \tag{3.1}$$

$P(u)$ can be interpreted as the price at time u, and X the output of the project, which depends only on its age. Also let C represent total capital cost, assumed constant and independent of time, and let r be the rate of interest. Then the net present value at the time of construction or inception, $Y(t)$ is:

$$Y(t) = \int_t^\infty P(u) X(u\text{-}t) e^{-ru} \, du - C e^{-rt} \tag{3.2}$$

In order to simplify the above expression, assume further that the rate of output is constant throughout, so that, without loss of generality, X' (u-t) can be set to equal unity. Now assuming differentiability, Y' (t) is the marginal net present value with respect to time, i.e.,

$$Y'(t) = -P(t)e^{-rt} + rCe^{-rt} \quad . \tag{3.3}$$

The first order condition for a maximum is that $Y'(t) = 0$, or

$$P(t) = rC \quad . \tag{3.4}$$

For example, Fig. 3.1 shows that NPV is negative at present; it becomes positive just after 1976, but goes on increasing until 1984, i.e., when the marginal net present value is zero. The optimal construction time in this example is then 1984.

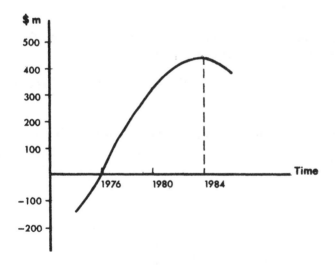

Fig. 3.1

In addition an absolute maximum requires that the second order condition be satisfied as well, i.e. $Y''(t) < 0$. In economic terms the first order condition means that the marginal loss in benefits (per unit of output) from further postponement just equals the marginal savings in interest costs; the second order condition means that the rate of increase of marginal revenue be less than the interest factor.

However, if it is assumed that P(u) is monotonically increasing for
all t, and that benefits are independent of project age, then the second
order condition is satisfied, and one need only rely on the first order
condition to derive the rule that

$$\frac{P(t)}{r} = C \quad . \tag{3.5}$$

This equation states that the optimal timing of investment is when the
present value of the benefits equals the cost of the capital outlay for
the *first time.*

The most important implication of the assumption of independence
of project age is that the static rule of equation (3.5) requires that
either projects last forever, or that they are replaced upon collapse[2],
since, by assumption, the benefit rate is increasing. This reduces the
investment decision to a choice of a single construction date: the
choice of the time at which to undertake the *first* of an infinite
sequence of identical projects.

Let the life of the project (plant) be n years, assumed constant. Then
the problem is to choose t so as to maximise:

$$Y(t) = \int_{t}^{\infty} P(u)e^{-ru} \, du - \sum_{i=0}^{\infty} Ce^{-r(t+in)} \tag{3.6}$$

and the optimising condition corresponding to equation (3.5) is:

$$\frac{1 - e^{-rn}}{r} P(t) = C \quad . \tag{3.7}$$

The above formulations contain the essentials of the timing problem
as seen by Marglin. But while concentrating on project age (finite or
otherwise), his treatment of demand is implicit: P(u) is 'determined by
the intersection of demand and supply functions . . .' (p.17). It is clear
that in any analysis over time, demand must be allowed to exert a more
explicit influence over investment decisions.

One way of incorporating demand is to consider the future plants
(in equation (3.6)) as catering for the growing demand over time, and
assume once again that past investments last forever. This reduces the
investment timing problem to the determination of a single time
interval when the additions to capacity are made. This is how Manne

[24] approaches the problem. However, in order to tackle the new dimension of demand over time, Manne simplifies the objective function. Since the total output added over all plants must equal the total demand target for each future point in time, the first term on the r.h.s. of equation (3.6) is dropped and so the objective function is simply to minimise all investment costs.[3] Because of its close relationship to the model developed in Chapter 4 below Manne's model is surveyed in some detail.

In its simplest static form, it resembles the make-or-buy model as shown by Fig. 3.2. For demand less than or equal to *0a*, the cost of internal manufacture exceeds the cost of outside purchase; beyond *a* it is cheaper to manufacture, due to the concavity (economies of scale) of the cost function, M.

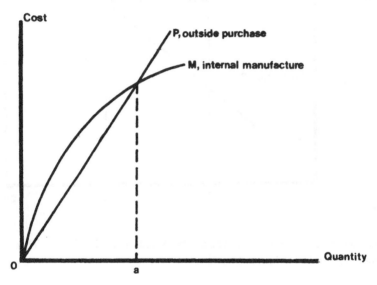

Fig. 3.2

When the same problem is posed in a dynamic framework a number of assumptions need to be made. As stated above, it is assumed that plant life is infinite, and that each new plant in the future is required to satisfy the increment in demand. Of course the economies of scale are a novel feature, but the timing problem is reduced to the determination of the constant time interval between plant construction. The economies of scale and demand increment determine the size of the plant. However, the determination of the constant time interval is connected to scale and demand because demand increment is defined per unit of time.

The assumption of constant time interval is called the assumption of constant cycle time. It is immediately obvious that it is this assumption which permits an infinite horizon (as in Marglin). In Fig. 3.3, constant cycle time is x, and is associated with arithmetic growth in demand,

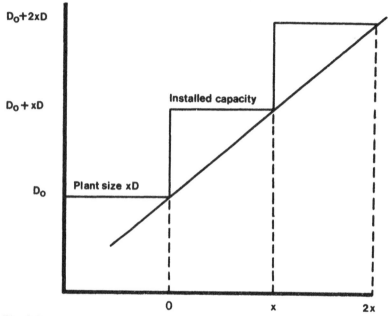

Fig. 3.3.

i.e., a constant increment in demand every year, say 20,000 tons. This model is now stated more formally.

Let D = annual increase in demand (tons/year)
x = time interval between successive plants (years).

Therefore

xD = plant size (tons/year)
$f(xD)$ = investment cost function for a single plant of size xD (dollars, say)
r = rate of discount

and let

C(x) = the sum of all present and future investment costs.

The present costs are of course $f(xD)$. After x years a further $f(xD)$ cost in incurred and its present value is $e^{-rx} f(xD)$. The total costs[4] can be written:

$$C(x) = f(xD) + e^{-rx}f(xD) + e^{-rx}f(xD) + \ldots . \qquad (3.8)$$

This infinite series can be written compactly as:

$$C(x) = \frac{f(xD)}{1 - e^{-rx}} \qquad (3.9)$$

The function $f(\cdot)$ is given a specific form which expresses the economies of scale as in Fig. 3.2.
Let

$$f(xD) = k \cdot (xD)^a \qquad 0 < a < 1 \qquad (3.10)$$

where k is a constant of proportionality.
Hence equation (3.9) becomes solvable:

$$C(x) = \frac{k \cdot (xD)^a}{1 - e^{-rx}} \quad . \qquad (3.11)$$

Now the function $C(x)$ in equation (3.11) has a unique minimum with respect to x and the minimum can be found by taking logarithms of both sides of equation (3.11), and setting the differential with respect to x to equal zero:

$$\frac{d \log C(x)}{dx} = \frac{a}{x} - \frac{r}{e^{rx} - 1} = 0 \quad . \qquad (3.12)$$

Since a and r are known, the optimal value of x, called x^*, is given in the relation

$$a = \frac{rx^*}{e^{rx^*} - 1} \quad . \qquad (3.13)$$

Optimal cycle time x* is then a function of *a* and *r*; for a given *r*, *x** is a decreasing function of the scale parameter *a*. The relationship is sketched in Fig. 3.4 below. It should be noted that economies of scale increase as *a* decreases. Hence the lower the value of *a*, the higher *x**. The relationship shown in Fig. 3.4 holds for a given rate of discount. As the rate of discount decreases, for a given value of *a*, *x** increases. Note also, that the solution of equation (3.13) exists if and only if $0 < a < 1$.

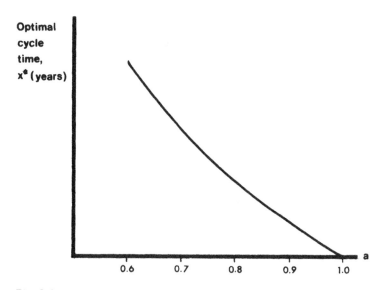

Fig. 3.4

The results show that the greater the economies of scale, the greater the optimal excess capacity,[5] as the interval between successive plants increases.

In short, Manne minimises investment costs over an infinite horizon; all operating costs are assumed to be proportional to output, i.e., there are no economies of scale in operating costs, and they are therefore left out.

The analysis can be extended to incorporate (a) geometric growth of demand, (b) time-phasing of imports with domestic production, and (c) multiple producing areas. (The last mentioned extension is not relevant to the models developed in the following chapters and therefore this aspect will not be discussed.)

A geometric rate of growth is easily incorporated; in Fig. 3.3, the straight demand line is replaced by an exponential curve. T.N. Srinivasan[6] shows that the constant cycle time model is approximately optimal: the use of arithmetic growth when demand is in fact geometric results in an increase in costs of not more than 3.16 per cent for $0.4 \leqslant a \leqslant 0.9$. Indeed, for the range of a from 0.6 to 0.9 the increase in costs does not exceed 1.13 per cent.

When the model is extended to include time-phased imports, the equations corresponding to equations (3.11) to (3.13) are more complicated, since in addition to x, there is another decision variable y, the time interval for imports, as shown in Fig. 3.5. However, Donald Erlenkotter[7] shows that y can be expressed as a function of x, so that the total cost is now $C(x, y(x))$, which can be minimised using dynamic programming techniques.

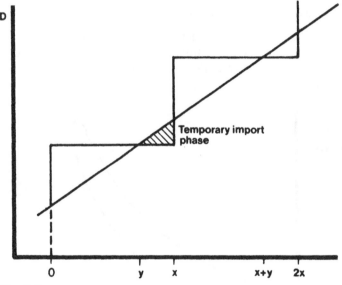

Fig. 3.5

It should be obvious that allowing a temporary import phase means that x* increases, which means larger capacities can be built after the import phase. Consequently, greater benefits (lower costs) can be derived from economies of scale by postponing construction of capacity for a specified period. A further consequence of the additional decision variable y is that excess capacity is no longer a necessary concomitant of investment problems with economies of scale. In other words, once imports are permitted, Chenery's 'permanent excess capacity hypothesis' need not hold any more. This is shown more explicitly in Manne's 1961 article [23].

Finally, there is one crucial assumption basic to the Manne-Erlenkotter models surveyed here, an assumption which is of course explicitly stated, namely, that initial capacity is equal to initial demand. The models are designed to answer the problem of capacity size and time-phasing for the next project to be built. Hence the issue is capacity expansion, in the strict sense. An implication of this assumption is that while the models are dynamic they are autonomous;[8] otherwise a variational form could not be avoided.

In the next section a verbal statement of the model to be developed in the next chapter is given, and is compared with the Manne-type models.

3.2 A Simple Model of Investment with Timing

Consider a country in which the demand for a commodity (steel)[10] is expected to grow geometrically from a given base (Fig. 3.6). Assume for a beginning that there are (1) no economies of scale and (2) no lumpiness[11] in investment.

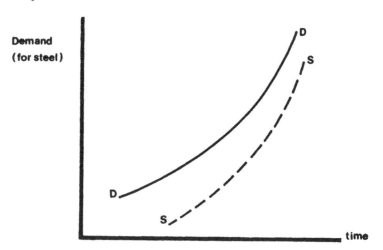

Fig. 3.6

Assume also that the concern of the public authorities is simply how to satisfy this demand.

When the domestic and world price of the commodity coincide, then equation (3.5) provides a valid rule for the timing of investment. The domestic supply curve, if positive at all, would be below the demand curve,[12] for example as shown in Fig. 3.6. At most the supply curve SS would coincide with the demand curve DD, signifying that the least cost policy is to satisfy demand every year with domestic production by a continuous expansion of capacity, year by year.

However, continuous expansion of capacity is not possible in practice because of 'lumpiness' in investment. This lumpiness can be characterised as follows: the initial lump for a minimum plant size is large, and subsequently larger 'balanced' plant sizes are discrete because of technical and physical constraints. For example, it may not be possible to design the entire production process in such a way that it produces (say) 10 MT of steel more per day. But not all the technically balanced and feasible plant sizes are worthy of economic interest. Indeed, the determination of the optimal plant size – for any given time, and for given initial conditions – is the object of the exercise. Thus it can be seen that the determinants of lumpiness are both technological as well as economic.

With the above definition of lumpiness, it follows that economies of scale imply lumpiness. This means both assumptions must be relaxed together. When the two assumptions are relaxed, the domestic supply curve is no longer like the one depicted in Fig. 3.6; it resembles the step function of Figs. 3.3 and 3.5. But not all the 'steps' are necessarily equal, since constant cycle time is not assumed. (In fact they are more likely to be unequal.)

From the discussion in Section 3.1, it follows that without the assumption of constant cycle time, the horizon will have to be finite. Also, the objective function will take a variational form. Optimal capacity will of course be a function of the fixed horizon, but for an industry in which technology is rapidly changing, commitments from now to eternity just do not make sense.[13] However some sensitivity of the results to changes in the horizon can be considered.

Apart from the fixed horizon, the objective function will be similar to the Manne-Erlenkotter model: all opportunity costs are minimised over the horizon. These opportunity costs, within a make-or-buy framework are: (1) all investment costs net of the value of terminal capital stock, and it is assumed, as in Manne, that larger plants cost proportionally less (i.e., there are economies of scale in investment costs);[14] (2) domestic production costs, which in contrast to Manne's approach, are a function of scale; and (3) imports. Since initial capacity is zero, there will always be some imports, at least during the gestation period.

In Chapter 9 the objective function is made parallel to a dynamic net benefit criterion, i.e., similar to equation (3.6), where the opportunity costs find a natural extension in social cost benefit analysis. In Chapter 10 some consideration will be given to the implications of the results for planning in practice.

Throughout demand growth is geometric, and imports (or output) are valued at world prices, and all valuations are in (constant) foreign exchange. The world price of the commodity (say steel) falls at a constant proportionate rate equal to the expected long run 'efficiency gain' in the industry, i.e., technological progress enters the model through a falling (real) price of steel. As mentioned before, all export possibilities are ruled out, although of course if export demand were known or could be forecast, it would be simple to increase the demand by that amount. Since this is a non-convex optimising problem, without demand as a datum, one would run into the same kind of 'paradoxes of infinity' that Manne[15] speaks of in his book.

Notwithstanding the fact that demand will be treated as being exogenous throughout, in principle it seems possible to incorporate the model within a more general macroeconomic optimum growth model, e.g., as in Weitzman [36]. In this work, the author formulates a two sector model. One sector produces a consumption/investment good under conditions of constant returns to scale. However, this output is constrained by the capacity of the second sector, infrastructure. Investment in the latter yields increasing returns to scale.

Weitzman's results have some interpretative value for development planning even when infrastructure investment is treated as a simple Manne-type problem and included into a general Ramsey-type framework.

A more general approach is given by Dixit, Mirrlees and Stern [11], where the problems associated with the introduction of economies of scale over the whole economy within an optimum growth model are analysed, and the 'paradoxes of infinity', mentioned earlier, are highlighted. As might be expected, some features of the solutions of the model of Chapter 4 are similar to the results obtained by Dixit, Mirrlees and Stern, e.g., infrequent investment. However, to repeat, their concern is with *macro*economic optimum growth policy whereas our main preoccupation is the dynamic optimisation of investment in a single sector where there are known economies of scale, and for which purpose demand can be taken as a datum.

In this chapter, by way of introduction, two important approaches to dynamic investment planning were surveyed. In Section 3.2 a dynamic investment planning model with economies of scale was presented in an informal manner, and some of its features which were common to the models in Section 3.1 were highlighted. In the next chapter the model is developed rigorously.

Notes

1. It should be noted that the survey is selected in the light of its relevance to the models developed in subsequent chapters; no general survey of dynamic investment planning is intended. Other models that would be of interest are surveyed in J.K. Sengupta and A. Sen [31]. Also excluded are aggregate investment planning models within the framework of macroeconomic optimum growth policy, e.g. those of Arrow and Kurz [2]. But see p.34 below.
2. I.e., independence of project age assumption is replaced by a 'one hoss shay' assumption.
3. Operating costs too are ignored, but the procedure is justified by Manne. See pp. 25-31 below for a discussion of Manne's model.
4. Manne and his fellow contributors use Regeneration Point Theorems to derive equation (3.9) above.
5. This result had been obtained by Chenery [9] previously. Chenery's result became known as the "Permanent excess capacity hypothesis".
6. T.N. Srinivasan [33].
7. Donald Erlenkotter [14].
8. A system is called *autonomous* if it is independent of initial time, i.e., it will take the same path whether it operated in the time interval (t_0, T) or $(t_0+1, T+1)$. See Pontryagin *et al.* [29], pp. 14-15.

   For example, firing a rocket from point A on earth to point B on earth (in minimum time, say) is a dynamic but autonomous problem. But firing the rocket from earth to the moon in minimum time is non-autonomous, since the relative positions of the two bodies depend on time (date) which must affect the trajectory of the rocket.

   Thus in Manne-type models, as long as we begin at "a point of regeneration" (i.e., a point in time when capacity is equal to demand), the solutions are the same. Otherwise the total cost function would have an additional argument, time.
9. Some formalisation and mathematical properties of Manne's model are studied in two papers by J. Jeskold-Gabszewicz and J.-P. Vial [20], [21]. In the main they are concerned with introducing capital depreciation and technological progress. The assumptions of constant cycle time and equality of initial capacity and demand are retained.
10. As the case study in Part Two deals with steel, from here onwards it will be convenient to refer to the commodity as simply steel.
11. Lumpiness is defined below.
12. It could be argued that in principle when the time for domestic production has arrived, the whole of demand must be satisfied by domestic production or not at all. For the purposes of this introductory analysis we can assume that an investment budget constraint or some other constraint might prevent us from satisfying the whole of demand initially.

13. See S. Chakravarty [7] on the merits of finite planning horizons.
14. The investigation is confined to constant elasticity investment cost functions. See Chilton [63] and Moore [27].
15. Manne [24], p. 31. The "paradox of infinity" is when optical capacity is infinite. In a practical computation, optimal capacity would be trivially the largest plant size the data incorporates.

4 AN INVESTMENT PLANNING MODEL WITH ECONOMIES OF SCALE

The previous chapter surveyed some approaches to the problem of dynamic investment planning. In this chapter an investment planning model with economies of scale is presented. As stated in the previous chapter, the model bears a close relationship to Alan Manne's approach, although there are some essential differences.

The model is first formulated in continuous time and presented in Section 4.1. In Section 4.2 it is made computable by reformulating it in discrete time. This requires that a functional recurrence relation be derived for the objective functional of the continuous time version, and that the constraints be discretised.

4.1 The Model in Continuous Time

4.1.1 Notation

All time arguments of variables are presented in round brackets (e.g., u(i)) for the discrete time version of the model. Its continuous time analogue is written with a subscript t, e.g., u_t.

- K = accumulated capital in million US $.
- $u(i)$ = amount of capital invested (in million US $) at the beginning of the ith stage. u is an *admissible* decision or *control variable.* The set of all u(i) is U, and is called the *control set.*
- $u^*(i)$ = the optimal u(i). The set of u*(i) is the *optimal policy.*
- $\overline{u}$ = the minimal (first) lump of investment (in million US $).
- $x(i)$ = production capacity, in thousand metric tons, of steel at stage i. x is an admissible *state variable.* The set of x(i) is X, called the *state space.* Q is a subset of X such that
  $$Q = [x(i) \mid x(i) \geq d(i)].$$
- $x^*(i)$ = an optimal x(i), [x*(i)] are determined by the optimal policy.
- $\overline{x}$ = the minimum positive capacity (in '000 MT), resulting from an investment of $\overline{u}$.
- $d(i)$ = demand for steel at time i, in metric tons (MT).
- $r(i)$ = domestic output per unit of time, in MT.

$m(i)$ = CIF import prices in \$/MT.

$c(i)$ = unit costs of production at time i. In general, $c(i) = c[x(i)]$, and are obtained as data.

$H(i)$ = the return function for stage i, to be minimised.

4.1.2. The Parameters of the Model

Time is represented as follows:

$[t_0, T]$ is the (finite) planning horizon; in the discrete version it is divided into N equal periods of unit length each representing a year, and t_0 is set to equal 1.

α = parameter of economies of scale, $0 < \alpha < 1$.

There is a one time period lag between investment and capacity creation. $\overline{u}$ leads to a capacity in the following time period to be $\overline{x}$ in '000 MT. All capacity is measured in '000 MT.

Δ = the interval between the elements $(\geqslant \overline{x})$ of X, the State Space.

It only applies to the discrete version.

[Of course Δ is also used to represent "a change in," i.e., as a differential operator. But there can be no confusion here.]

$\overline{u}$, α and $\overline{x}$ are technologically given.

The remaining parameters are:

a_1 = initial demand for steel in '000 MT

a_2 = initial import price, CIF, in US \$/MT

β = rate of growth of demand

σ = rate of growth of prices

λ = rate of discount

b = a constant, $0 < b < 1$

G = a constant, $G \geqslant 2.0$

T' = fixed life of a plant (in years)

4.1.3 The Objective Functional[1]

The problem may be stated as follows:

Given the exogenous growth in the demand for steel, to investigate whether capacity for domestic steel production should be created; if it is to be created, then how should it be time-phased so that it is optimal in a dynamic sense. The phasing of capacity must be such that advantages of economies of scale — inherent in the process industries — are exploited.

The standard form of the objective functional is to maximise net benefits (see Chapter 3). It was also shown in that chapter that when certain conditions hold, the minimisation of costs (as in Manne's formulation) would be sufficient. But when there are, in addition, economies of scale in production costs, the maximisation of net benefits is the appropriate specification of the objective functional.

However, there are computational advantages in formulating the problem as one involving minimisation, and it turns out that if 'sacrifices' are suitably defined, then the minimisation of sacrifices is equivalent to the maximisation of net benefits, when demand is a datum.

Let the sacrifices be the sum of all expenditures of capital, imports and the costs of production.

In symbols the problem is:

$$\min_{u_t} J = \int_{t_o}^{T} [u_t + [d_t - r_t] m_t + C_t - V_T] e^{-\lambda t} dt \tag{4.1}$$

subject to

$$u_t = A(x_{t+1} - x_t)^\alpha, \quad 0 < \alpha < 1 \tag{4.2}$$

where

$$A = \frac{\overline{u}}{\overline{x}^\alpha} \tag{4.3}$$

and

$$x_{t+1} - x_t \geq \overline{x} \qquad \text{or} \qquad 0 \tag{4.4}$$

$$K_t = \int_{t_o}^{t} u_\tau d_\pi, \qquad K \geq 0 \tag{4.5}$$

$$d_t = a_1 e^{\beta t} \tag{4.6}$$

$$m_t = a_2 e^{\sigma t} \tag{4.7}$$

$$r_t = \min(d_t, x_t) \qquad r_t \geq 0 \tag{4.8}$$

$$C_t = b \, r_t \, m_t + G.c_t x_t \tag{4.9}$$

$$x \in X \quad \text{and} \quad u \in U \tag{4.10}$$

$$x_T \in S(x_T, T) = 0 \tag{4.11}$$

$$x_{t_0} = 0 \quad \text{given} \tag{4.12}$$

$$V_t = \Delta x_i \int_T^{i+T'} e^{-(\lambda+\sigma)(t-i)} \left[m_T - \frac{C_T}{x_T} \right]_+ dt \quad . \tag{4.13}$$

Furthermore, it is reasonable to require that

$$c_t > 0 \quad \text{iff} \quad x_t > 0 \tag{4.14}$$

$$r_t > 0 \quad \text{iff} \quad x_t > 0 \quad . \tag{4.15}$$

4.1.4 Discussion

Each of the above equations is now discussed in some detail. First equation (4.1) is the objective functional. It minimises all sacrifices of investment expenditure, plus the cost of imports, plus the total domestic costs of production, minus the terminal value of the capital stock, all in present value terms over the entire horizon. Note that domestic production is valued in foreign exchange (i.e. at the CIF import prices in US $) and enters the objective functional as a negative quantity. Demand in excess of domestic production is imported, but the model does not preclude zero domestic production, if indeed that course minimises all sacrifices.

Equations (4.2) to (4.4) should be considered together. Equation (4.2) is the basic 'capital-to-capacity' relation. It is based on the empirical evidence on economies of scale and is used in a number of studies.[2] Equation (4.3) gives a productivity index, based on a single observation of the 'capital-to-capacity' curve for the process under consideration. (Later on the productivity index A is allowed to change with time.) Equation (4.4) states that the production capacity can be increased by building another plant, but that the new plant cannot be smaller than the currently available minimum plant size.[3]

Equation (4.5) is simply an identity. However it could easily be treated as an annual investment budget constraint, if capital rationing were to be introduced.

Equations (4.6) and (4.7) state that demand and prices grow exponentially. In the absence of better long-run forecasting models, the simplest projections seemed best. The deterministic treatment of demand and prices is also somewhat at odds with real life observations; however, it did not seem that making demand and price stochastic would add to the degree of realism.[4]

When the price exponent σ in equation (4.7) is positive this implies either (a) that the real price is increasing or (b) that the real cost of foreign exchange is rising for the country in question. When σ is negative, it implies that the real price is falling, or that the real cost of foreign exchange is falling. *A priori*, one would expect that in a competitive world the rate of fall of real price would be equal to the rate of technical progress.

Equation (4.8) states that domestic output is set by demand or capacity, whichever is the lower. This in fact suppresses what could have been another decision variable.

Equation (4.9) gives the total costs of production. The first component varies with output, the second with scale. In general, c_t is a declining function of capacity, x, and it taken as datum for the purposes of the model.

Equation (4.12) states that initial capacity is known and that it is zero. No terminal constraint, such as that terminal capacity should be equal to or be greater than demand, is specified. In the terminology of variational problems, there is a necessary 'natural boundary condition' at x_t, but no terminal point. The latter means that the problem could not be solved by classical variational methods unless some terminal surface — like equation (4.11) — were given.

Equation (4.13) gives the value of terminal capital stock. The basic motivation is to value terminal capital in terms of the value of net output it will generate beyond the horizon. It is clear that such a valuation procedure carries over the benefits of economies of scale into the valuation of terminal capital. Net output is estimated by the difference between the unit (import) price at terminal time and the average unit cost of production. Strictly speaking, one should make the unit cost a function of time as well (to reflect the 'age of the plant'). However, such a procedure makes the integration quite complex,[5] and it was felt that equation (4.13) can be used as a workable approximation, especially as it leads to a computationally manageable expression — as shown below.

First for notational simplicity, let

$$\frac{C_T}{x_T} = \overline{c}_T \quad .$$

Then integrating equation (4.13) and rearranging gives:

$$V_T = \Delta x_i \frac{m_T - \bar{c}_T}{\lambda + \sigma} \left[e^{-(\lambda+\sigma)(T-i)} - e^{-(\lambda+\sigma)T'} \right] . \tag{4.16}$$

It will be apparent from the next chapter that the above expression for the terminal value of capital can be incorporated quite straightforwardly into the computational algorithm.

Finally equations (4.14) and (4.15) are self-explanatory. In the next section the model presented here is discretised.

4.2 The Model in Discrete Time

In this section the model consisting of equations (4.1) to (4.15) is discretised and presented within the framework of Dynamic Programming. Two additional restrictions are required to make the model computable.

The framework of Dynamic Programming relies on Bellman's Principle of Optimality which is illustrated in Fig. 4.1. But first consider any four points A, B, C, and D on a surface. Quite simply stated, the principle states that the shortest (optimal) path from A, through points B and C, to D contains the shortest (optimal) path from B to D and from C to D. In Fig. 4.1, the principle is illustrated for a single state variable. The curve $x^*(t)$ for $t_0 \leqslant t \leqslant t_1$ is the trajectory associated with the optimal control with given initial and terminal states. The trajectory is divided into two parts: (1) and (2) at time τ. According to the Principle of Optimality, trajectory (2) defined for

x = State Variable

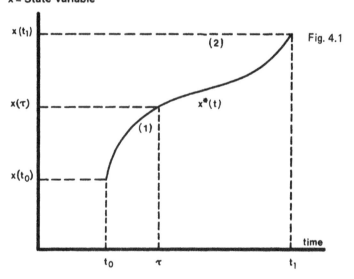

Fig. 4.1

$\tau \leqslant t \leqslant t_1$, must in its own right represent an optimal trajectory with respect to initial condition $x(\tau)$. This is furthermore independent of how the system arrived at the initial conditions for the second portion.

The most direct proof of the principle of optimality is given by Aris [1]. The proof is compelling in its simplicity, for economists anyway, and is worth quoting. It is a proof by contradiction:

> If you don't do the best with what you happen to have got, you'll never do the best you might have done with what you should have had.

The principle reduces the problem to a sequence of decisions and is the fundamental justification for a functional recurrence relation which is derived below.

Equation (4.1) is a function of x_t, u_t, and time, and so adopting the notation appropriate for discrete time,[6] it may be written more generally as follows:

$$\min J = \int_{t_0}^{T} F(x(t),\ u(t),\ t)\ dt \tag{4.17}$$

with the initial value of x given by

$$x(t_0) = x_0 \ . \tag{4.18}$$

The minimum will be a function of the initial t value t_0 and the initial x value x_0. Equation (4.17) may now be embedded within a family of functions by introducing the function:

$$f(t_0, x_0) = \min J \ . \tag{4.19}$$

Since the integral of equation (4.17) has the additive property

$$\int_{t_0}^{T} = \int_{t_0}^{t_0 + \Delta} + \int_{t_0 + \Delta}^{T} \tag{4.20}$$

the principle of optimality can be utilised to give:

$$f(t_0, x_0) = \min \left\{ \int_{t_0}^{t_0 + \Delta} F(x(t), u(t), t)dt + \underline{f}\ [(t_0 + \Delta), x(t_0 + \Delta)] \right\} \tag{4.21}$$

Now $[T - t_0] = N$, the number of time periods of unit length. Since this information is also embedded it is convenient to write $f(t_0, x_0)$ as $f_N(x_0)$.

Taking $\Delta = 1$, equation (4.21) becomes:

$$f_N(x_0) = \min \left\{ \int_{t_0}^{t_0+1} F(x(t), u(t), t)dt + f[(t_0+1), x(t_0+1)] \right\} . \tag{4.22}$$

Consider the first term on the r.h.s. of equation (4.22). Without loss of generality t_0 can be set to equal 1. In this case the integral equals the return from the first time period, or as it will be referred to from here on, the first *stage*:

$$\int_1^2 F(x(t), u(t), t)dt = H(1). \tag{4.23}$$

Now recall equation (4.2) given in section 4.1, which — with appropriate notation — is:

$$u(i) = A(x(i + 1) - x(i))^\alpha . \tag{4.24}$$

This equation can be written more generally as:

$$x(i + 1) = g(x(i), u(i), i) . \tag{4.25}$$

In the light of equation (4.25), it is clear that the second term on the r.h.s. of equation (4.22) can be written

$$f_{N-1} [g(x(i), u(i), i)] \tag{4.26}$$

And substituting (4.23) and (4.26) into (4.22) yields the functional recurrence relation:

$$f_N(x_0) = \min_{u(i)} \left\{ H(1) + f_{N-1} [g(x(i), u(i), i)] \right\} \tag{4.27}$$

where $g(.)$ represents equation (4.24) and

$$\begin{aligned} H(i) = & [u(i) + [d(i) - r(i)] m(i) + br(i)m(i) \\ & + G \cdot c(i)x(i) - V_T] e^{-\lambda(i-1)} \end{aligned} \tag{4.28}$$

and subject to the rest of the (discretised) equations:

$$u(i) = A_0 (x(i + 1) - x(i))^\alpha \tag{4.24}$$

where $\quad A_0 = \dfrac{\overline{u}}{\overline{x}^\alpha} \tag{4.29}$

and

$$x(i + 1) - x(i) \geqslant \overline{x} \text{ or } 0 \tag{4.30}$$

$$K(i) = | \sum_{\tau=1}^{\tau=i} u_\tau \quad K(i) \geqslant 0 \tag{4.31}$$

$$d_t = a_1 e^{\beta t} \quad \text{becomes} \quad d(i + 1) = a_1(1 + \beta)^i \tag{4.32}$$

$$m_t = a_2 e^{\sigma t} \quad \text{becomes} \quad m(i + 1) = a_2(1 + \sigma)^i \tag{4.33}$$

$$r(i) = \min(d(i), x(i)) \quad r(i) \geqslant 0 \tag{4.34}$$

$$C(i) = br(i)m(i) + G \cdot c(i)x(i) \tag{4.35}$$

$$x \in X \mid X = [0, \overline{x} + k\Delta, \ k = 0, 1, 2, \ldots] \tag{4.36}$$

$$u \in U \tag{4.37}$$

$$\text{Let } Q \subset X \mid Q = [x \geqslant d(T)] . \tag{4.38}$$

Then we require that

$$\max x(T) = \min Q \tag{4.39}$$

and

$$x(1) = 0 \text{ given.} \tag{4.40}$$

$$V(T) = \Delta x(i) \frac{m(T) - \overline{c}(T)}{\lambda + \sigma} [e^{-(\lambda+\sigma)(T-i)} - e^{-(\lambda+\sigma)T'}] \tag{4.41}$$

where

$$\overline{c}(T) = \frac{C(T)}{x(T)} \quad \text{(as before)}$$

and finally

$$c(i) > 0 \quad \text{iff} \quad x(i) > 0 \tag{4.42}$$

$$r(i) > 0 \quad \text{iff} \quad x(i) > 0 . \tag{4.43}$$

4.2.1 Discussion

Equations (4.27) to (4.43), together with (4.24), constitute the complete investment planning model analogous to the continuous time version of equation (4.1) to equation (4.15), given in section 4.1 of this chapter. The exact correspondence between the discrete version and the continous time version, as well as the new features are now discussed.

First, it must be clear that equations (4.27) and (4.28) together correspond to the objective functional, given in equation (4.1). The validity of the functional recurrence relation (4.27) rests on the principle of optimality.

Second, equations (4.24), (4.29), and (4.30) correspond respectively to (4.2), (4.3), and (4.4), which have already been discussed. Third, equations (4.31) to (4.35) correspond respectively to equations (4.5) to (4.9) and are quite straightforward. The only difference is that they are now written with the notation reserved for the discrete version.

It is in fact equations (4.36) to (4.39) that contain the new features which are basically (a) the specification of a discrete state space, and (b) a limitation on terminal capacity.

Equation (4.36) states that the state space X is a grid of x-values. That is, the first admissible value of x is zero, the second $\overline{x}$, the third $\overline{x} + \Delta$, the fourth $\overline{x} + 2\Delta$, and so on. The upper bound on the state space is given by equation (4.39), on which more later. The value of Δ can be set depending on accuracy requirements, and in practice also by the available computer store.

Equation (4.37) states that u is an element in the control set U, which is generated by equations (4.24), (4.29), and (4.30). The first element of U is zero, since x may be zero. It is obvious from these equations that the next value of u is of course $\overline{u}$, the investment required for the smallest available plant of size $\overline{x}$.

Equation (4.38) specifies a subset Q of X, such that all x in Q are greater than or equal to terminal demand. Equation (4.39) then states that the largest admissible terminal capacity will be the smallest element of Q. This equation exploits the constraint placed on domestic output $r(i)$ – see equation (4.34) or (4.8). Since output never exceeds demand, the search for optimal capacity need not exceed the first 'available' capacity that is greater than or equal to terminal demand.

It should be noted, however, that this does not mean that *optimal* capacity should necessarily be equal to terminal demand; indeed optimal capacity can be less than terminal demand, or even zero. Equation (4.39) simply puts an upper bound on the state space X. Nor is it a terminal constraint in the strict sense; it simply reduces the search procedure and terminal capacity is itself subject to optimisation.

Finally equation (4.40) states that initial capacity is given as zero. The remaining three equations are self-explanatory: equation (4.41) gives the terminal value of capital, and the remaining two correspond to equations (4.14) and (4.15).

To sum up, in the discrete version a functional recurrence relation was first obtained, and then a suitable restriction was imposed on the (discrete) state space by specifying the largest admissible capacity.

The complete model made up of equations (4.24) and (4.27) to (4.43) will be called *Model One* throughout this book. Model One is applied to the case study in Part Two and some computational results are given in Chapter 8.

4.2.2 Model Two

Model Two differs from Model One in that in Model Two technological progress and efficiency gains are introduced. This means that only two equations are affected.

First, equation (4.3) becomes equation (4.44):

$$A_t = \frac{\overline{u}}{\overline{x}^\alpha} e^{\sigma t} \tag{4.44}$$

and equation (4.9) now becomes:

$$C_t = br_t m_t + (c_t x_t) e^{\sigma t} \tag{4.45}$$

Writing these two equations in discrete form is quite straightforward and is omitted.

First consider equation (4.44). In this equation σ is used as a proxy for the rate of capital-saving technical progress. For the long-run, this may not be too bad as an approximation.

Equation (4.45) introduces an efficiency gains parameter in the domestic production of steel, and it is assumed that over the long-run this efficiency gains parameter will approximate the long-run rate of fall in the real price of imported steel.

Some implications of the two assumptions of Model Two are discussed in Chapter 8.

This completes the formal presentation of the investment planning models. In the next chapter some computational aspects are discussed.

Notes

1. A note on terminology is perhaps appropriate here. When the domain of a real valued function is a set of functions, it is referred to as a functional. Thus in equation (4.1), J is a functional. But, of course, the optimised value of J, call if J*, is a function; it is a function of initial parameters. This terminology is used throughout.
2. See for example, Manne [24], Weitzman [36], Dixit, Mirrlees and Stern [11].

3. Some limitations of this and other assumptions are discussed in Chapter 8.
4. In fact, Manne [23] found that making demand stochastic lead paradoxically
   to increased investment, and excess capacity in his optimal solutions.
5. It seems that in such a form, some approximating technique would be required
   to complete the integration.

4 COMPUTATIONAL ASPECTS OF THE MODEL

In this chapter section 5.1 gives a brief description of the Dynamic Programming algorithm. Section 5.2 sets out the full computational procedure with the aid of a flow chart that formed the basis of the computer code.

5.1 A Computational Algorithm

As noted in Chapter 2, the central feature of dynamic programming algorithms is to embed a particular problem into a wider class of problems characterised by certain parameters and then the Principle of Optimality is used to obtain a fundamental recurrence relation.

When time enters in an essential way into the problem, 'backward sequencing' will capture the irreversibility of time. However, backward sequencing does require two simplifying assumptions:

1. That the time-horizon (or the number of 'stages') be finite,[1] and
2. That no 'decision' (or investment) be made in the terminal year.

Now for concreteness assume that the particular problem is what decisions should be made over the time-horizon, given a state at the start. Note too that each decision en route will 'transform' the state. This requires finding a particular time path of decisions for the particular starting point or state. The technique of dynamic programming is to find all the possible paths from any possible starting point. If all these paths are now known, then clearly the particular path is known too.

This no doubt sounds like the brute force of combinatorial analysis, and if this was all, then there would be little to recommend dynamic programming. It is here that the Principle of Optimality comes in and drastically reduces the task.

The algorithm begins by exploiting the two assumptions stated above. First, as a result of a number of past decisions, in the terminal year, T, one could be in any one of a number of such states. (Obviously, the number of such states must be finite — more will be said later on this.) Associated with each possible state, there will be a sum of costs, or benefits, or simply the 'return' for being in that state.

Clearly the same set of states is also possible for the year T−1, as a result of past decisions. Consider Fig. 5.1. The return associated with the first state x(1) in year T−1 is added to the return associated with the same state in year T, and then with the next state x(2), x(3), and so on, and the minimum (maximum) noted. Also noted is the corresponding optimal transition, with which there is an associated

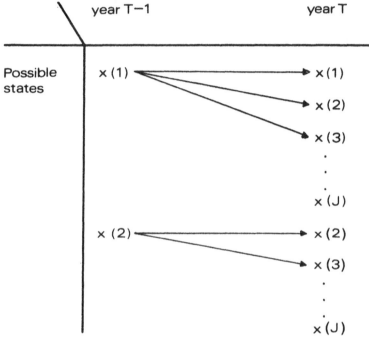

Fig. 5.1

decision. Next, the same stepwise optimisations are considered for the remaining possible states in year T−1.

Now the two-year cumulative return plays the same role, as did the return associated with the terminal year, and we now consider year T−2, T−3, etc. until we reach the present.

In this way the full optimal time path (and of course the associated optimal decisions) for any initial state is known, and so the particular path, say beginning with x(1) in year 1, is also known.

As stated above, the number of possible states has to be finite. Since for the model in question the states are in fact capacities, it means that the spectrum of capacities under consideration must be finite − which is quite reasonable. Indeed, if there was information on the available plant sizes, say if the set of balanced plant sizes was smaller, the set of x's (called X in Chapter 4) could be suitably restricted.

Depending on accuracy requirements and the available computer store, it would be possible to make the set X quite large (but finite). The number of x's in X is called a 'grid', and the interval between x's the 'grid size'.[2]

Since accuracy depends on grid size, the following point, made by Bellman and Dreyfus ([4], p.88) is worth stating. Their point is illustrated with a diagram similar to Fig. 5.2. With any discrete grid there is the theoretical possibility of missing a sharp optimum between x_2 and x_3 (in Fig. 5.2), though the computational procedure will pick up the minimum (assuming we are minimising) at x_4. However, Bellman and Dreyfus point out that such a drastic example is unlikely in practice. But obviously the danger increases as the grid gets coarser.

Also, the use of a discrete grid imparts a certain 'stability' to optimal solutions to some ranges of variations in some parameters, while optimal solutions show certain 'jump' characteristics for very small variations in other parameters. This point should be borne in mind when considering the sensitivity results given in Part Two.

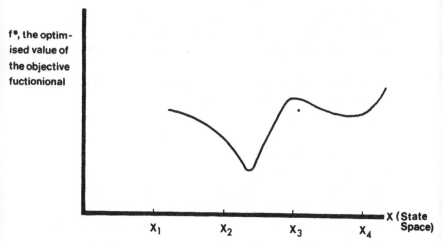

Fig. 5.2

Consider the following three grid points:

x_1 . . . . . . | / / / / / /x_2/ / / / / / | . . . . . .x_3

Suppose x_2 is an optimal x. Any variation of parameters which leaves the optimum within the shaded range (equidistant from x_1 and x_3) will still show x_2 as an optimal x. The jump to x_1 or x_3 only occurs when the optimum is closer to x_1 or x_3.

Since in the model demand grows with time, the set of admissible capacities – or the state space – also increases with the time horizon. In order to build up a sensible picture of optimal policies, a horizon of up to 30 years will be considered in the following chapters.

Finally, it is perhaps worth noting that the functional recurrence relation relies on Bellman's Equation, which is a *necessary* condition for an optimum. In theory, therefore, one is assured of a local optimum only. In practice, however, since an explicit algorithm for minimisation is used, the optimum is in fact a global one[3] – subject to the possibility of a sharp optimum between grid points (discussed above with the aid of Fig. 5.2).

5.2 The Computational Flow Chart

In this section the computational procedure is outlined with the aid of Chart 1. The steps given below refer to the steps marked on Chart 1. As the chart is self-explanatory, the commentary below is brief.

Step 1: First the basic data are read in, and the prices and demands for the entire time-horizon are generated and stored.

Step 2: The state space (or the grid) is generated and stored. As noted before, the maximum element of the state space just exceeds demand in the terminal year.

Step 3: The purpose here is simply to reserve store for a matrix of optimal capacities to be obtained later. The matrix is called NX(I, J), where I refers to the year, and J identifies the capacity, or X.

Step 4: The algorithm begins here, with the terminal year, say year 20. There is no investment in the last year: the capacity in the last year can only be a result of past decisions, and so the return function is evaluated for each element J of the state space – which leads to a 'column' vector of the return function called FOLD(J).

Step 5: This is the core of the algorithm. Store an arbitrarily large
number in a location called RLOC. We move to a year 'previous' to
the terminal year, i.e., to year 19. The first possible capacity in year
19 (as indeed in any year) is X(1) which is zero. Taking capacity as
zero, the return function is evaluated for the year 19. This is added
to FOLD (1). This sum cannot possibly exceed the amount in
RLOC, and it then replaces what was in RLOC before. The X value
in question goes into NX(19, 1).

Now the return function is evaluated as follows: let capacity in year 19
remain zero (or X(1)) and add to it the return function in year 20,
assuming the next possible capacity, X(2). Is this less than FOLD(1)?
If so, it *becomes* FOLD(1), and X(2) goes into NX(19,1). This
procedure is continued until all the step-wise transitions for the years
19 and 20 have been considered. In the matrix NX is stored the
information that for *any* 'initial' condition (i.e., capacity) in year 19,
the optimal transition to year 20 is known.

Next, years 18 and 19 are considered in the same way that years 19
and 20 were considered. Then years 17 and 18, 16 and 17, and so on
until years 1 and 2 have been considered in the same manner. (This is
the Principle of Optimality at work.)

Step 6: Here one simply traces the path of the optimal capacities
stored in matrix NX(I, J), beginning with the initial capacity in year
1, which is in fact zero.
Step 7: It follows that if the optimal 'state' to be in for each year is
known, the optimal decisions for each year are also known, starting
from year 1 to year 20. Now it is a simple matter to evaluate a
cumulative return function over the optimal path, starting from year
1 to year 20.

To sum up: the essential irreversibility of time is preserved by
backward sequencing. The particular optimal path is really a by-
product; we in fact have all the optimal paths for any possible initial
capacity, as a result of the embedding of the particular problem into a
wider class of problems.

In Part Two a case study of dynamic investment planning is
considered in detail and the models developed in Chapter 4 are applied.

Chart 1: Flow Chart for Computing the Model (Model Two)

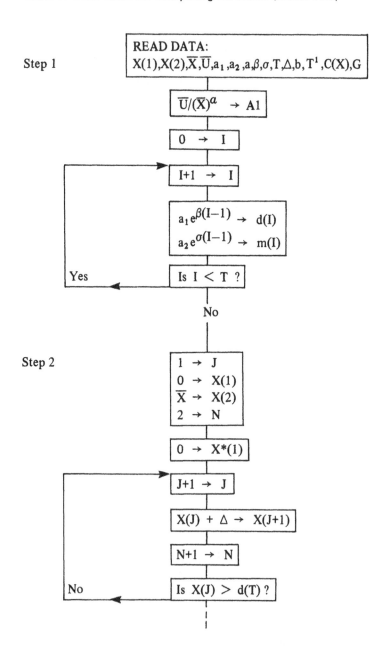

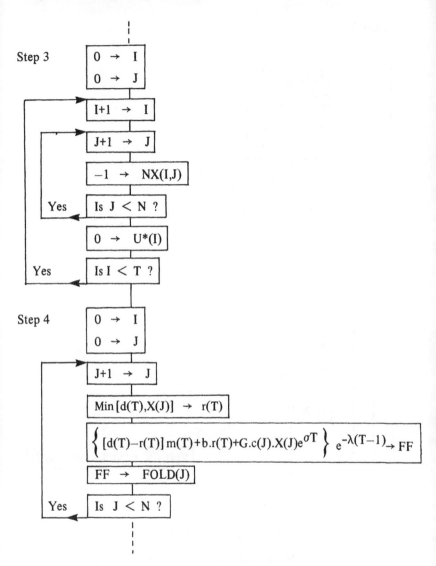

Step 5

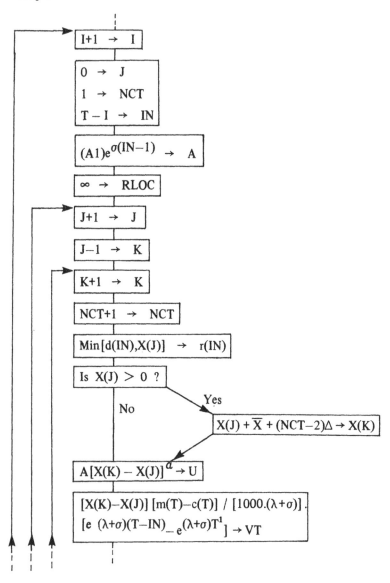

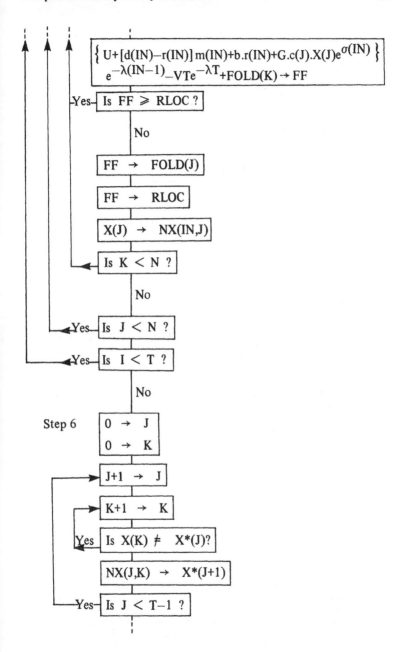

$$\left\{ U + [d(IN) - r(IN)]\, m(IN) + b.r(IN) + G.c(J).X(J)e^{\sigma(IN)} \right\}$$
$$e^{-\lambda(IN-1)} - VTe^{-\lambda T} + FOLD(K) \rightarrow FF$$

Yes — Is $FF \geqslant RLOC$?

No

$FF \rightarrow FOLD(J)$

$FF \rightarrow RLOC$

$X(J) \rightarrow NX(IN,J)$

Is $K < N$?

No

Yes — Is $J < N$?

Yes — Is $I < T$?

No

Step 6
$0 \rightarrow J$
$0 \rightarrow K$

$J+1 \rightarrow J$

$K+1 \rightarrow K$

Yes — Is $X(K) \neq X^*(J)$?

$NX(J,K) \rightarrow X^*(J+1)$

Yes — Is $J < T-1$?

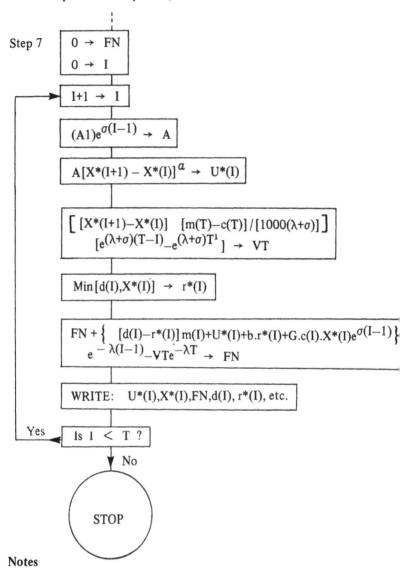

Step 7

$0 \to FN$
$0 \to I$

$I+1 \to I$

$(A1)e^{\sigma(I-1)} \to A$

$A[X^*(I+1) - X^*(I)]^a \to U^*(I)$

$\left[\, [X^*(I+1)-X^*(I)] \, [m(T)-c(T)]/[1000(\lambda+\sigma)] \, \right]$
$[e^{(\lambda+\sigma)(T-I)} - e^{(\lambda+\sigma)T^1}] \to VT$

$Min[d(I),X^*(I)] \to r^*(I)$

$FN + \Big\{ \, [d(I)-r^*(I)] \, m(I)+U^*(I)+b.r^*(I)+G.c(I).X^*(I)e^{\sigma(I-1)} \Big\}$
$e^{-\lambda(I-1)} - VTe^{-\lambda T} \to FN$

WRITE: $U^*(I), X^*(I), FN, d(I), r^*(I)$, etc.

Yes

Is $I < T$?

No

STOP

Notes

1. For infinite horizons, Bellman and Dreyfus [4] discuss two types of convergent iterative procedures. These are 'approximations in policy space' and 'approximations in function space'. They are both very complex trial-and-error methods and can claim vast amounts of computing time.
2. For the case study, annual capacity in iron- and steel-making is usually reckoned in thousands of MT. Thus in all the computations reported in Part Two, grid size is 10,000 MT, i.e. $\Delta = 10$. In actual practice, it is most unlikely that a capacity 'expansion' of less than 10,000 MTPY would be considered.

3. In practice, the problem of distinguishing between a local and global optimum will arise only when optimising with respect to two or more decision variables. This is because the computation usually takes the form of optimising over one variable y_1, then over another variable y_2, then again over y_1, and so on. This procedure usually converges to a relative optimum, depending on initial guesses. However, it may still be possible to obtain a number of relative optima—one then hopes that the global optimum is among these. Examples of this kind are discussed in Bellman and Dreyfus [4], pp. 82-3, and 89-96.

PART TWO: APPLICATION

6 PLANNING A STEEL INDUSTRY

Part One of this book was devoted entirely to theoretical aspects of dynamic investment planning. To this end the relevant literature was surveyed in Chapter 3. In the following chapter planning models were formulated with mathematical rigour. The models were designed to reflect some real characteristics of industrial plants so that the models are as close to reality as possible. The actual mathematical technique used to solve these models was introduced in Chapter 2 and the computational aspects discussed in Chapter 5.

In Part Two a detailed application of the above theory is given. The planning of a steel industry is considered as a case study. For only a thorough application of a case study can demonstrate the operational validity of the theoretical part of this book. However, as noted in Chapter 5, dynamic programming solutions are a function of initial parameters and small variations in these can show rather large changes in optimal policies. It is thus most important to establish the initial parameters with extreme care, as far as it is possible to do so. A fairly wide ranging sensitivity analysis is also essential to test the 'robustness' of solutions. These two issues will therefore dominate Part Two.

In this chapter the planning of a steel industry is placed into a certain context. This is important because no planning problem can be properly treated in the abstract.

At the minimum, the planner interested in the steel industry would require information on (a) technology of steel production and (b) international trade in steel; the former including *process routes* of steel production and their viability, minimum and maximum plant sizes, and technological change, and the latter comprising the major trade flows, the nature of the international market and how these affect the parameter estimates. As for prices, capital and production costs, it seems best to gather these together in the next chapter which deals exclusively with the parameters required for computation. Section 6.1 is a brief discussion of the changing nature of iron and steel technology. Section 6.2 covers the relevant aspects of international trade in iron and steel.

6.1 Steel Technology

In the mid 1850s the invention of the Bessemer converter and the open-hearth steel-making processes made the mass production of steel an economically viable industry.[1] For nearly half a century the Bessemer method dominated steel production until, around 1905, it lost its leadership to the open-hearth method. Fifty years later, the oxygen-blown furnace was introduced for large-scale production and is now the most widely used steel-making process in the industry and is generally referred to as the blast furnace-basic oxygen system, BF-BOS. All these methods involve a two-stage process in which iron ore is first converted to liquid iron or hot metal, which is then refined to yield steel.

The first commercial application of an alternative process, in which the intermediate product takes the form of solid sponge iron instead of liquid iron was in 1957 in Monterrey, Mexico. This was a direct reduction (DR) process.[2] However, two important technological developments in the conventional BF-BOS route have helped to maintain its competitive edge over the alternative method. These were reductions in coke consumption and increases in the size of the blast furnace and steel-making vessels.

In 1950, blast furnaces in the UK required about 1,030 Kg of coke per tonne of hot metal; in Japan the figure was 900 Kg per tonne. In 1972 the UK requirement fell to just over 600 Kg per tonne and in Japan to under 450 Kg per tonne.[3]

The second important development was the economies of scale gained by increasing the size of each production unit both in the iron-making and steel-making processes. The output of the largest blast furnace (for iron-making) has increased by a factor of 4 over the 12-year period, 1960-72, that is, from just over 100 MT per working hour to over 450 MT per working hour. The output of the largest basic oxygen furnace (for steel-making) has also increased by a factor of 4 over the same period (i.e., from 100 MT per working hour to 375 MT per working hour), although it seems that the physical limit is now being reached for steel-making vessels.

But quite apart from the physical factors, the continued growth of world steel production via the blast furnace would imply doubling the demand for coking coal by the end of the century. It is unlikely that such a scale of demand could be met, even if newly discovered deposits in Canada and Australia are taken into account. This combination of factors has led to the interest in DR processes in the developed world.

While the DR processes are in their early stages of development, the scale of production is small, and since they are also less capital-intensive than the BF-BOS route, the techniques seem to be suitable for developing countries with a relatively small scale of demand. However, since the DR processes share the so-called 'cubic dimension' properties[5] in common with the BF-BOS route, there is every reason to believe that the scale of the DR processes will continue to increase in the future.

Direct reduction is simply the stripping of the oxygen component of ferrous and ferric oxide. This is done by a reducing agent or a reductant, which may be a gaseous reductant (e.g., natural gas) or a solid reductant (coal, electricity, nuclear heat).

The DR processes produce sponge iron, and the degree of reduction (i.e., percentage of Fe content) determines the next stage in the process. When ore has an Fe content of between 30 per cent and 70 per cent, it is simply called 'prereduced iron', which can be used in the production of pig iron. When the degree of reduction is very high, i.e., around 90 per cent Fe, it is charged into an electric arc steel-making furnace. (The entire route can be abbreviated to DR-EF.) The higher the quality of the ore (in terms of Fe content), the more suitable it becomes for DR processes, from the technical point of view.

DR processes using natural gas to produce sponge iron (i.e., over 90 per cent Fe) are:

1. Hyl
2. H-Iron
3. Midrex (also called 'Midland-Ross')
4. Fior
5. Futakuski
6. Armco
7. Purofer

Only the first two were in commercial operation in October 1973, the remainder were all in pilot stages.

DR processes using solid reductants (coal or coke) are:

1. SL-RN
2. Krupp-Renn
3. Hoganas
4. Echevarria
5. Elkem
6. Nueve process

According to a UNIDO Secretariat document,[6] seven plants to produce prereduced ore based on solid reductants were established in the 1960s; three of these have now been permanently closed down due to technical problems. A further eight sponge iron plants based on solid reductants (i.e., three SL-RN plants, one Krupp-Renn, two Hoganas, one Echevarria, and one Nueve process) have been in operation. Of these, one SL-RN plant and the Echevarria plant have closed down permanently; one SL-RN plant has proved to be non-viable after three years; three others only began production in 1972 or 1973 and so nothing can be said about their viability yet. This leaves only two small plants (Hoganas[7]) in Sweden, which have been operating since 1911.

The document concludes that DR processes based on solid reductants have not yet proved their technical or economic viability and that these processes should be the subject of further research. To the future also belongs a solid reductant technology based on the reduction of iron oxide by hydrogen derived from water with the use of nuclear power (E.W. Voice and J.M. Ridgion [81]).

The chemistry of gaseous DR processes is simple.[8] First, natural gas (CH_4) is reformed by thermal-catalytic cracking to produce the reducing gas according to the following reactions:

$$CH_4 + H_2O = CO + 3H_2$$
$$CH_4 + CO_2 = 2CO + 2H_2$$

The reducing gas is then passed through the furnace containing iron ore or iron oxide pellets to produce the following reactions:

$$Fe_2O_3 + 3H_2 = 2Fe + 3H_2O$$
$$Fe_2O_3 + 3CO = 2Fe + 3CO_2$$

The sponge iron is then charged to an electric arc steel-making furnace to complete the DR-EF route. The liquid steel goes to a continuous casting machine to produce billets, which finally end up in the rolling mill.

In 1969 four Hyl plants were in commercial operation in Mexico and it was reported that by April 1972, 24 countries were considering Hyl installations.[9]

In October 1973 there were four Midrex plants in operation although the first such plant only began producing in March 1972 in Hamburg, Germany. Consequently, no operational data exists (apart from data pertaining to pilot conditions) to compare their economic performance with that of Hyl installations.

To sum up, direct reduction technology not only allows countries endowed with high quality iron ore to consider utilising their resources in the production of steel but it also emerges as a possible alternative route for the major producers when coking coal costs become prohibitive. To quote R.S. Barnes [61]:

In the long term, the direct reduction-electric arc furnace route could become the major route to steel, for it is in this way that nuclear energy is most likely to be harnessed to steel-making.

6.2 International Trade in Iron and Steel

6.2.1 Iron Ore

Before considering international trade in steel, the pattern of world production and trade in iron ore is outlined. Table 6.1 shows the rising share of developing countries in the production of iron ore.

Table 6.1: Global Production of Iron Ore in 1955, 1970 and Estimated Capacity in 1975 (in millions of MT)

	1955		1970		1975	
	MT	%	MT	%	MT	%
Global Total:	372	100	753	100	925	100
North America	121	32	136	18	172	19
Western Europe	118	32	133	18	141	15
Eastern Europe	79	21	210	28	233	25
Asia	21	6	88	12	110	12
Latin America	17	5	78	10	114	12
Africa	12	3	62	8	65	7
Australia	4	1	46	6	90	10

Source: J.R. Miller [69].

If we assume that most of Eastern European ore will be used or traded within COMECON, then on the basis of the 1975 estimates the developing countries will account for over 40 per cent of iron ore available to the Western world. As one would expect, the changes in the production pattern are reflected in a growth in the share of internationally traded ore. In 1960, 30 per cent of world output was internationally traded; in 1970 this rose to 33 per cent. According to a UN study,[10] this growth in the international trade is expected to continue. The principal trade flows in 1970 were (a) from Canada and Latin America to the US; (b) from Scandinavia, Africa and Latin America to Western Europe; (c) from the USSR to the Eastern European countries; and (d) from Australia, Asia and Latin America to Japan.

The most important factors that contributed to the increase in trade are (a) depletion of easily accessible ores and the depletion of high quality ores in Western Europe, (b) increases in the size of ocean freighters and (c) developments in the technology of beneficiation and iron ore concentration, a factor which is perhaps more important than the other two mentioned above.

In the technology of iron ore preparation perhaps the most striking developments are *sintering* and *pelletisation*. (These are both methods of 'agglomeration' – for a lucid exposition of these terms, and the processes of iron ore preparation, see J.R. Miller [69].) As a blast furnace charge both sinters and pellets are equally acceptable. Pellets, however, handle better in transportation and contain more value-added than sinters. For this reason developing countries – which as has been shown, will become important sources of iron ore – would favour pelletisation. Indeed, if the policy of increasing value-added is taken a step further, then various qualities of directly-reduced ore (including 'prereduced' ore) would increase their share in internationally traded iron ore. The development of the DR-EF route, and its wider use would certainly encourage that trend.[11] Table 6.2 shows the relative importance of sinter, pellets and directly-reduced ore and forecasts to 1985.

Having highlighted the role of the developing countries in the supply of iron ore, it seems possible that with the formation of the Iron Ore Exporters' Association (along the lines of OPEC, CIPEC and IBA), the developing countries might have a decisive voice on price policy, on agglomeration and/or degree of direct reduction of exported ore.

6.2.2 Steel

The most striking change in the pattern of steel production has been the decline of the share of US production in world output and the dramatic increase in Japanese production. In 1950, the US share was 50 per cent; in 1955, it fell to 30 per cent, and by 1970, to 20 per cent. In contrast, the Japanese share of world output was 4 per cent in 1955 and rose to 16 per cent in 1970.

Table 6.2: Physical Form of Iron Ore Consumed in the World in 1970 and Forecasts to 1985 (in millions of MT)

Form	1970		1975		1980		1985	
	MT	%	MT	%	MT	%	MT	%
Screened Ore	298	39.5	332	36.3	357	33.1	395	31.6
Sinter	346	46.0	402	44.3	463	42.8	500	40.0
Pellets	106	14.1	165	18.2	196	18.2	231	18.5
Directly-reduced Ore	3	0.4	11	1.2	64	5.9	124	9.9
Total:	753	100.0	910	100.0	1080	100.0	1250	100.0

Source: J.R. Miller [69]

World steel production in 1970 and forecasts to 1985 by regions is given in Table 6.3.

In 1960, the developing countries accounted for 6 per cent of world production, 3 per cent of world consumption, and their imports amounted to 55 per cent of their consumption. However, in 1968, this ratio of imports to consumption fell to 28 per cent, due to rapid developments in Latin America and Asia.

In contrast to the trade in iron ore, international steel trade is very much a marginal activity, except perhaps for trade in specialised steels among OECD countries. The following shares of exports as a

Table 6.3: World Crude Steel Production Forecasts (in millions of MT)

	1970[a]		1975		1980		1985	
	MT	%	MT	%	MT	%	MT	%
World Total:	592.2	100	735	100	915	100	1025	100
North America	131.7	22	149	20	170	19	181	17
Western Europe	161.1	27	174	24	219	24	243	24
Eastern Europe	154.6	26	187	25	227	24	256	25
Asia[b]	119.6	20	169	23	212	23	241	23
Latin America	13.0	2	28	4	43	5	49	5
Africa and Middle East[c]	5.4	1	9	1	13	1	18	2
Oceania[d]	6.8	1	19	2	31	3	37	4

a. Actual production
b. Asia includes China, India and Japan. In 1970, Japan alone produced 16 per
    cent of world steel output.
c. Main producer Republic of South Africa.
d. Main producer Australia.

Source: J.R. Miller [69].

proportion of production in 1968 is instructive:

USA	4%
ECSC	23%
UK	17%
Japan	13%

Even in the early 1970s, Japanese exports as a proportion of their
production did not exceed 15 per cent.

L. Friden [65], who has studied international trade in steel, found
considerable evidence of double pricing. He found that in the period
1953-1968, prices for home markets (i.e., domestic prices) were very
stable, partly due to state intervention and partly due to an
oligopolistic production structure. On the other hand, export prices
were continuously subject to supply and demand.

Friden obtained a measure of the differences in the two prices by
calculating the unit value of exports to countries *outside* the ECSC and
the unit value of deliveries *between* ECSC countries for the period
1955-67. The figures below show the limits within which the estimated
ratios varied:

Wire	0.88 − 1.14
Merchant bars	0.82 − 1.09
Heavy and Medium Plates	0.92 − 1.29

The estimates suggest that considerable price differences have
occurred between domestic market prices and export prices, where the
latter sometimes exceed the former and at other times were well below
it.

The Japanese steel industry has also practised double pricing. The
comparable limits are even wider:

Merchant bars	0.73 − 1.37
Heavy sections	0.73 − 1.49
Heavy plates	0.69 − 1.59

Furthermore, the Japanese data shows that in 1957 export prices exceeded domestic prices by as much as 40-60 per cent.

No export prices for the UK are available but, in general, these were in line with those of the ECSC. Thus, if ECSC export prices are compared with UK domestic prices for the period 1956-67, the following range of ratios is obtained:

Merchants bars	0.65 – 1.35
Wire	0.64 – 1.23
Heavy sections	0.64 – 1.48
Heavy plates	0.67 – 1.70

These figures can be contrasted with those for the US for the same period:

Merchant bars	1.04 – 1.10
Heavy sections	1.04 – 1.10
Heavy plates	0.98 – 1.10
Cold rolled sheet	0.98 – 1.11

If one takes into account that the US export prices probably included an element of transport costs, then it seems that export prices deviate from domestic prices by no more than 5 per cent. Friden therefore concludes that US producers did not practise double pricing.

The role of the ECSC in export trade suggests that, given its dominant position, it often acted as price leader, with the UK and Japan following the lead. Indeed, this is not surprising since (as Friden states) export cartels and official price cooperation existed during the period 1953-68 in the ECSC, Japan, Sweden and the UK.

Thus Friden concludes that during 1953-68:

> . . . more than four-fifths of world production was sold at prices the stability of which stands out in stark contrast to the fluctuations of the international steel trade. The world trade in steel could therefore be described as a marginal market on which the absence of regulations and other imperfections of the market facilitate considerable variations in price and quantity.

The corollary is that domestic prices were shielded from international competition so that wide differences between domestic prices of the various countries persisted, as shown in Table 6.4.

Table 6.4: Price Index of Merchant Bars in 1966 (ECSC Export Price = 100)

ECSC (export price)	100
Australia (domestic price)	115
Japan (domestic price)	124
Sweden (domestic price)	127
UK (domestic price)	143
USA (domestic price)	188
Brazil (domestic price)	214

Source: Friden [65], p. 47.

6.2 Conclusion

The aim of this chapter was to place the investment problem within an international context. Direct reduction processes are likely to grow in importance both in the developed and the developing countries, and if the dominant energy source of the future is nuclear fission, then the future technology of steel is DR-EF. If the major producers of the world continue to prefer high grade ores, then international trade in ore will grow. Since most of this ore comes from developing countries, a tendency to increase the value-added component in exported ore can be expected. This will suit the major steel producers too, since one way of satisfying their larger tonnage requirements is to increase the Fe content per MT of imports.

International steel trade is small as a proportion of world output. For strategic reasons, the developed countries of the West as well as the East will continue to support their own steel industries.[12] And, because the advantages of a steel industry are location-specific,[13] each developing country is likely to want a steel industry of its own if it has good iron resources.[14]

Notes

1. UN/ECE, Comparison of Steel-Making Processes, United Nations, New York, 1962 [77].
2. Patents have been granted for over a hundred direct reduction processes, but only a few have reached the stage of commercial application.
3. While it is difficult to forecast how low coke consumption can get, W.F. Cartwright [62] quotes that (in 1968) the theoretical limit could be as low as 390 Kg per tonne of iron, a limit which is not far off in Japan.
4. R.S. Barnes [61].

5. 'Cubic dimensions' refer to the fact that while material cost of equipment varies with surface area, capacity is determined by the volume enclosed. This is a fundamental justification of technological economies of scale. As economies of scale are a crucial aspect of the study, it is covered in detail in the next chapter, where estimates of the scale coefficient are also given.

6. UNIDO Secretariat (Sept. 1973) [80].

7. No further information on the process or on the two Swedish plants was available.

8. I.A. Mozer and G.H. Laferriere [71].

9. R. Lawrence (1972) [67].

10. A. Marelle [68].

11. The unreliability of steel scrap supplies and its widely fluctuating prices also means that producers prefer sponge iron as a "sweetner" to scrap.

12. Extrapolating the present trends in increases in the size of the blast furnace, R.S. Barnes estimates that by 1985, 13 blast furnaces could supply the entire demand of the EEC. See R.S. Barnes [61].

13. UN/ECA, *The Development of an Iron and Steel Industry in Africa*, Addis Ababa, 1963, [34].

14. Witness the collapse of the two proposed Western African and Eastern African Iron and Steel sub-regions.

7 THE REQUIRED PARAMETERS AND THEIR ESTIMATION

In the previous chapter it was stated that the planning of a steel industry will be chosen to demonstrate the operational validity of the planning models developed in Part One. However, it is perhaps well to note that the method is equally applicable to any process industry of manufacturing industry, for almost all manufacturing industries worthy of planning display certain common characteristics:[1] economies of scale in investment costs or production costs or both; discrete plant sizes with a minimum and a maximum size, but with histories of fairly rapid technological change which may or may not be measurable, and so on.

For any possible case study, the problem must be further particularised so that it emerges as a concrete example of the usefulness of the theory. The theory will be applied here for the planning of a steel industry for Zambia. This is in fact a real life problem where, as shown below, both the timing and scale of the investment was much debated. The models when applied to Zambian data will determine the optimal timing and scale of steel plants for Zambia, together with the optimal import strategy.

It was emphasised earlier that because optimal policies depend on initial parameters, these will have to be well established.It is the function of this chapter to establish these data for use in the computations of models reported in the next two chapters. Section 7.1 deals with prices and economies of scale; 7.2 deals with costs; and 7.3 covers demand estimates and its projections.

7.1 Prices and Economies of Scale

7.1.1 Prices

The longest series of steel export prices available is that for merchant bars. (The export prices of all other primary forms of steel, like plates, sections, etc., moved in line with the price of merchant bars. See, for instance, *The Iron and Steel Industry in 1972 and Trends in 1973*, OECD, Paris, 1974 [73].) The cyclical pattern of the prices is shown in Table 7.1. Since, in the investment planning model, domestic output as well as imports are valued at the 'world price' of steel, the long term change in the real price of steel is of crucial importance. Evidence of

Table 7.1: Export Price of Merchant Bars, 1913-73 (Price[a] in US $ per MT; Index 1953 = 100)

Year	Price	Index
1913	$ 24.90	
1929	27.90	
1939	41.75	
1950	65.20	
1953	93.85	100
1954	84.85	90
1955	101.30	108
1956	109.45	117
1957	128.00	136
1958	105.00	112
1959	81.50	87
1960	112.00	119
1961	100.00	107
1962	95.00	101
1963	70.50	75
1964	80.00	85
1965	91.00	97
1966	83.00	88
1967	78.00	83
1968	•78.00	83
1969	79.00	84
1970	127.00	135
1971	106.00	113
1972	116.00	124
1973	177.00	189

a. Annual average f.o.b. price, excluding taxes, quoted by continental producers; Bessemer quality steel.

Sources for prices: (1) World Trade in Steel and Steel Demand in Developing Countries, UN/ECE, 1968 [78]; (2) OECD Reports on the Iron and Steel Industry, 1964-73 [73].

Table 7.2 Average Annual Rate of Increase in the Index of Crude
Steel Output per Manhour, 1960-1967

	Annual Rate
EEC as a whole	5.9%
Belgium-Luxemburg	5.2%
West Germany	4.8%
Japan	14.2%
USA	3.6%

Source of Index: Cockerill and Silberston [64], p.33.

technical change and efficiency gains would be of interest here, for in
spite of export price cartels, the scale of fluctuations in export prices
(Table 7.1) is so immense and the export market so small that it is
unlikely that efficiency gains were not passed on to the importers to
some extent.[3]

It is clear from the data that no simple trend line can be fitted over
the whole series. Using the two observations 1953 and 1973,
one obtains an annual proportionate rate of growth of 3.2 per cent.
Since there is a cyclical pattern, a 'peak-to-peak' approach (1957 and
1973) gives a proportional annual rate of 2.1 per cent.

Now the general rate of inflation of OECD export prices over the
recent past, i.e., 1966-73, is around 5 per cent p.a. (see Dore, [13],
for details of regression equations). This means that the *long term real
export price* is falling at an annual rate of 2 per cent or 3 per cent.
It would be interesting to compare these rates with the evidence on
efficiency gains in the iron and steel industry.

Another independent set of data is provided by the International
Bank for Reconstruction and Development in a paper[3] that forecasts
price changes for all internationally traded commodities, including steel
and copper. According to this paper, over the period 1972-85, the real

Table 7.3: Average Steel Prices[a] per MT for Zambia

Year	KWACHA/MT	US $/MT
1973[b]		300.00
1972	N/A	N/A
1971	128.65	180.11
1970	132.51	185.51
1969	115.40	161.56
1968	109.81	153.73
1967	115.35	161.50
1966	107.45	140.63
1965	110.46	154.64
1964	112.83	157.96

a. Zambian imports are valued f.o.b. or f.o.r. depending on whether the goods are transported on sea or land. K1 = US $1.55.
b. Assuming same rate of percentage increase as that observed in continental export prices between 1971 and 1973, namely 66.98 per cent (see Table 7.1)

Source: *Annual Statements of External Trade, Rep. of Zambia 1964-1971* [39].

price of steel will fall at 2 per cent p.a. However, it also forecasts that the real price of copper will fall at 1.5 per cent p.a. over the same period. Since copper is Zambia's main foreign exchange earner — and is likely to be so for some time yet — it seems sensible to take this into account, so that effectively, on the basis of IBRD data, the real price of steel falls at 1/2 per cent p.a., for Zambia.

In Chapters 8 and 9 both sets of data will be used in the computations of the model. The first set will be simply called OECD data, and the second, IBRD data.

Finally, a base price for a tonne of steel imported into Zambia for the year 1973 is needed. Table 7.3 gives the average price of steel per MT on the basis of import statistics.[4] The $300 estimate for 1973 is f.o.b.; to this must be added 12 per cent for ocean transport[5] and a further $21 per MT transport inland to the Zambian border.[6] This gives a 'border price' of $357 per MT.

This figure can be checked against an independent source. The largest single importer of steel in Zambia made contracts for the supply of steel during 1973, at an average price of $386 per MT — the average takes the commodity composition into account. The evidence thus seems to point to a base price in excess of $350 per MT. However, in order to guard against a possible fall in the export price in the near future, a base price of $300 per MT is used in Chapters 8 and 9.

7.1.2 Economies of Scale

Haldi and Whitcomb [17] have summarised the available empirical evidence on economies of scale. Let the cost function be $C = bX^{\alpha}$, where C is the cost, b a constant, α the scale coefficient, and X the capacity. Estimating the equation for a sample of 662 pieces of industrial equipment,[7] Haldi and Whitcomb find that over 56 per cent of the estimates of α lie in the range of 0.50 to 0.79.

When the same equation is estimated for economies of scale over complete plant investment costs, 58 per cent of the estimates of α lie in the same range, i.e., 0.50 to 0.79.

Evidence of economies of scale in the steel industry has been recently summarised and presented in Cockerill and Silberston [64]. Of course the scale coefficient can be expected to vary with the process route. For the fully integrated BF-BOS route, the above mentioned authors find $\alpha = 0.56$ for the range of capacity between 0.1 million MT and 5 million MT for the UK.

Since the process under consideration here is the DR-RF route, likely estimates of the scale coefficient α for this route is an obvious necessity for the computations of Chapters 8 and 9. Unfortunately I was unable to find any estimate of α for the entire route, and perhaps it does not exist. A somewhat piecemeal approach is used here to obtain some estimates. Iron-making is considered first.

7.1.2.1 Iron-Making

A preliminary approach, on the basis of first principles, would suggest that given the description of the reduction plant, the 'six-tenth' rule holds, i.e., $\alpha = 0.6$. A number of economists have relied on this rule, especially after it was established by Chilton [63] over a wide range of plants used in the process industries.

A second approach is to estimate the elasticity between the highest and lowest plant sizes. The capital cost range quoted in the literature was $42-$51/MT for one million MT plant. The ENERGOPROJEKT Report [43] gives the capital cost of the reduction plant as $18.01 million, for an annual output (of sponge) of 0.215 million MT.

Now α, the elasticity, can be estimated as follows:

$$\alpha = \log(X_2/X_1)/\log(Y_2/Y_1) \tag{7.1}$$

where X_2 is the capital cost at the higher plant size; X_1 is the capital cost at the lower plant size; and Y_2 and Y_1 are the upper and lower plant capacities respectively.[8] This yields the following estimates of α for capacity between 0.215 million MT and 1 million MT:

Upper limit of capital cost ($51/MT)   ... α = 0.61
Lower limit of capital cost ($42/MT)   ... α = 0.55 .

7.1.2.2 Steel-Making

The scale coefficient for steel-making in the capacity range of 0.1 million MT to 2.5 million MT can be obtained from data given in Cockerill and Silberston [64], Table 38, p. 86. Their table is reproduced in Table 7.4, together with estimates of α, using equation (7.1). However, there is one drawback which would prevent one from taking the estimated values of α to be directly applicable to the DR-EF route. As stated by Cockerill and Silberston (p. 74), their data pertains to the following route:

Scrap (Iron and Steel) → EF → (Ingot) → Rolling Mill

In the UK some 98 per cent of electric arc furnace output is first cast into ingot moulds. The ingots are then reheated and passed through a primary rolling mill to produce billets, which are then rolled into the required final products.

However, in the DR-EF route, continuous casting by-passes the primary rolling stage: liquid steel is cast directly into billets.

Table 7.4: Estimates of Unit Costs at Different Output Levels of Crude Steel by Semi-Integrated Plants in the UK Producing Bars Only and Estimates of Scale Coefficient α

Process and Class of Cost	A Annual Crude Steel Output (Millions of MT)				α^c
	0.1	0.5	1.0 Unit costs in US $	2.5	
	(1)	(2)	(3)	(4)	
Steel-making					
Capital [a]	5.6	4.10	3.74	3.43	0.83
− index	163.6	119.6	109.1	100.0	
Operating[b]	22.8	17.52	16.73	16.58	0.61
− index	133.7	105.6	100.9	100.0	
Total	27.8	21.62	20.47	20.01	0.60
Rolling					
Capital[c]	25.06	10.03	10.03	10.03	0.48
− index	250.0	100.0	100.0	100.0	
Operating[d]	18.0	18.0	18.0	18.0	−
− index	100.0	100.0	100.0	100.0	
Total	43.06	28.03	28.03	28.03	0.58
− index	154.0	100.0	100.0	100.0	
TOTAL					
Capital	30.68	14.13	13.77	13.46	0.50
− index	228.0	105.0	102.0	100.0	
Operating	40.18	35.52	34.73	34.58	0.64
− index	116.0	103.0	100.0	100.0	
Total	107.68	86.47	85.32	84.86	0.62
− index	127.0	102.0	101.0	100.0	

Source: For Columns 1-4, Cockerill and Silberston [64], Table 38, p.86.

(For footnotes, see following page)

Table 7.4 Footnotes:

a. Calculated from the formula

$$K = [n.49400 M 2/3 + 108 Q + 2640 Q 2/3] \ i$$

where K = total capital cost in £, converted to US $ at £1 = $2.40
       n = number of furnaces in installation
       M = vessel standing capacity in MT
       Q = weekly throughput of installation in MT
       i = an inflation multiplier with a value of 1.16

Values of parameters are:

Annual Capacity (million gross MT)	Q	M	n
0.1	2083	52	1
0.5	10415	130	2
1.0	20830	180	3
2.5	52075	186	7

and assume approximately 40 taps a week, 48 weeks a year. Annual depreciation and interest are calculated at 15 per cent of the original investment.

b. Calculated using the formula

$$R_Q = [\frac{n.108000}{Q} + 96] \ i$$

where R_Q = operating cost per MT of product in shillings; n and Q have the same value as above, and $i = 1.25$.

Depreciation and interest are calculated as above.

c. Assumes combinations of bar mills with individual capacities of 0.25 million MT annually and with capital costs of £6 million each.

d. Operating costs for a bar mill of 0.25 million MT annual capacity.

e. Calculated between the lowest and highest output scales, using equation (7.1).

As continuous casting is more efficient,[9] this will raise the economies of scale (i.e., reduce α) at the rolling stage. Thus, the α values at the rolling stage underestimate the scale coefficient that one would expect for the DR-EF route.

The empirical evidence on the economies of scale may be summed up as follows:

1. Economies of scale not only exist, but are significant in the demand range of 0.1-1.0 million MT; the validity of the specification of the models in Chapter 4 rests on this fact.

2. All significant economies of scale in the rolling of shapes (as opposed to flats) are concentrated within a much lower range: 0.1 million MT to 0.5 million MT.

3. On *a priori* grounds, one would expect the scale coefficient in the reduction plant to be about 0.6, and the limited data available supports this view.

4. As the economies of scale in electric steel-making are not exhausted[10] within the demand range under consideration, the scale coefficient in iron-making (itself dominated by the scale coefficient of the reduction plant) will determine the scale coefficient of the entire DR-EF process, i.e., it will emerge as the 'least common denominator'.

5. Taking all the available evidence into account, the six-tenth rule seems to be a good approximation for the DR-EF route under consideration. Accordingly, the computations in the next two chapters will be based on the estimate of α being 0.6.

7.2 Production Costs

Since Zambia has acquired patent rights to install an Hyl plant, it would be of interest to consider the capital and production costs of the process.

The Hyl plant is suitable for small levels of demand ranging between 200,000 MT to 1,650,000 MT. Latest (May 1973) estimates suggest that the capital cost of 350,000 MT plant of reduced iron may be between $47 to $57 per MT and for 1 million MT installation between $42 and $51 per MT. (The corresponding capital cost range for solid reductant DR processes is $42-$51 per MT and $38-$46 per MT for plant sizes of 35,000 MT and 1 million MT respectively. But, as already mentioned, the commercial viability of such processes have not yet been proved.)

The comparative total production costs per MT of crude steel for a plant size of 1/2 million MT per year are given in Table 7.5. The figures in the table are based on the assumption that 'all processes are equally operable regarding ore and fuel inputs, site location, market, labour and supervision, financial support, and management' (see J.R. Miller [69], p. 43). The estimates therefore pertain to a hypothetical plant only: if all materials, etc., were equally available, at the assumed prices, then BF-BOS is still the cheapest route, provided output is not less than 1/2 million MT. The table should therefore be treated more as an indicator of relative resource use than as evidence of absolute superiority or a ranking of the three techniques.

The operating cost figures already given in Table 7.4 give an idea of the economies of scale in production costs. However, this data refers to scrap which is charged into an electric arc furnace the output of which

Table 7.5: Production Costs per MT of Crude Steel by Various Routes (Plant Size: 500,000 MT PY)

	BF-BOS		SOLID DR-EF		GASEOUS DR-EF	
	$	%	$	%	$	%
Raw Material						
Iron ore	15.60	26	18.50	29	18.50	26
Coal	15.50	26	9.70	15	–	–
Limestone	1.05	2	0.50	–	0.35	–
Scrap	2.05	4	2.05	3	2.05	3
Additions	1.65	3	1.65	3	1.65	3
		61		50		32
Iron-Making Conversion						
Electricity	0.12	–	0.43	2	0.32	–
Gas	–	–	–	–	8.25	–
Oil	–	–	0.12	–	–	–
Labour	0.77	–	0.60	–	0.90	1
Other	1.68	3	1.40	2	2.45	3
(Cumulative Conversion %)		64		54		48
Steel-Making Conversion						
Energy	1.28	3	6.65	10	6.65	9
Labour	1.80	3	1.92	4	1.92	3
Other	1.68	3	4.03	7	4.03	6
General Services	2.90	5	4.80	7	7.35	11
Iron-making	9.10	15	5.00	8	9.58	14
Steel-making	5.37	9	6.40	10	6.40	9
TOTAL PER MT OF STEEL:	$60.55	100	63.75	100	70.40	100

Price assumptions for above:
Iron ore (60% Fe) – Lump	$12.50/MT	Scrap	$34.00/MT
Iron ore – Fines	9.00/MT	Electricity	0.01 per Kwh
Coal: coking	24.00/MT	Natural Gas	0.48/1000 cf
non-coking	15.50/MT		

Other assumptions:
Scrap in steel-making charge	27%	Fixed charges	17%

Source: J.R. Miller [69].

is cast into ingots, which are then rolled. With DR-EF the costs of production that can be achieved in practice depend on a number of technical factors and it is virtually impossible to isolate their relative importance. Among these technical factors that influence the cost of production are:

1. presence of impurities in the iron ore, notwithstanding its high Fe content;[11]
2. the quality of pellets produced and their size distribution;[12]
3. economies in gas consumption;[13]
4. the time devoted to regular maintenance work; and
5. the degree of metallisation of sponge iron which has to be technically optimised.[14]

All these, and many other factors together contribute to the efficiency factor of the plant − when the full rated annual capacity of the plant is achieved, the efficiency factor is 1.0.

The computations in the following chapters are based on production cost estimates given by J.R. Miller [69] and the ENERGOPROJEKT Report [43], which was a feasibility study for Zambia. The use of the equation that represents costs of production, i.e., equation (4.35), is explained in the next chapter. The point that must be noted here is simply this: the production cost per MT of steel falls with the scale of output.

7.3 Demand Projections

The initial level of demand in MT (for the base year 1973) as well as its projected rate of growth are both crucially important for the computations of the following chapters. It is therefore necessary to consider demand in somewhat greater detail than the other parameters discussed so far.

Interest in the development of an Iron and Steel Industry in independent Zambia began with the publication of the UN/ECA/FAO Report [56] on the eve of Independence. The report, which has formed the basis of Zambia's Development Plans, lists an iron and steel complex among the possible manufacturing projects and recommends that a detailed feasibility study be undertaken.

Even since then the crucial demand for iron and steel has been subject to controversy. The first major feasibility study, undertaken by Bechtel Corporation,[15] was commissioned in November 1968 and presented early in 1971.[16]

The report identified demand as the most important constraint that made an integrated iron and steel plant financially unviable at that time. On the basis of import statistics it put demand, in 1965, at 109,000 MT. Yet on the basis of a market study[17] by Dr. Simonda of Indeco[18] undertaken in December 1968 it was concluded that iron and steel demand in 1974 for finished steel products would be 5,000 MT of pig iron and 54,500 MT of steel made up as follows:

    24,500 MT bars and rods
    10,000 MT angles
    17,000 MT strip
     3,000 MT channels and joists
    ————
    54,500 MT

In terms of crude steel demand, this is equivalent to about 78,000 MTPY, and the report recommended that an integrated iron and steel plant be deferred until crude steel demand rises to 120,000 MTPY. It added that at the current rate of growth of demand (assumed to be 4.5 per cent p.a.) the target demand would not be reached before 1985.

The report's financial projections were based on capital and operating costs and loan terms offered by suppliers. It was on strict commercial profitability criteria that the project was considered unviable. It conceded that further analysis 'to incorporate socio-economic factors' was necessary. This was done by Williams and Young [57] applying a social cost benefit framework to Bechtel's financial projects, which merely confirmed Bechtel's recommendations. The Zambian Cabinet shelved the project in 1971.

In August 1973, ENERGOPROJEKT, of Yugoslavia, produced their 'Feasibility Study for an Integrated Steelworks in Zambia' [43]. (The Energoprojekt Report does not state when the work was commissioned.)

This Report relied on a market study carried out by Mindeco,[19] although a section of Mindeco disagreed with this market study which they considered overestimated the demand for steel and called for yet another market study.[20] The first will be called the *Mindeco Study*. The second was carried out jointly by Indeco and Mindeco and so it will be referred to as the *Indeco-Mindeco Study* [45].

The Mindeco study began with a questionnaire sent out to 63 steel-using firms of which only 18 (or about 29 per cent) furnished the required information.[21] However, the study claimed that even this was an improvement over simple import statistics which, it was alleged, understated imports. Thus on the basis of the information gathered from the firms, it estimated demand (imports) for 1972 to be 162,103 MT. On examining the commodity composition of this study, it is clear that this figure is based on the SITC category 67 only, whereas it seems that at least SITC nos. 691 to 694 should be included. A later memorandum suggested that the true figure was probably in the 150,000-180,000 MT range. It should be noted that this is an estimate of finished steel and is equivalent to about 220,000 MT of crude steel.

The Indeco-Mindeco study was undertaken because it was argued that in the years 1970 and 1971 there had been some stockpiling of steel and that it was necessary to establish 'normal' annual consumption. It attempted to do this by producing a very detailed list of steel products by size and type. But the list itself was confined to what might be called 'standard stock items' by steel merchants. For instance, the list does not include any structural steelwork or iron and steel for bridgework. But the report does provide very useful information for the (proposed) mill on the exact sizes and shapes of steel products that should be rolled for immediate delivery to the market.

The study arrives at a total of 119,000 MT of *finished* products for 1972, and allows a 7 per cent p.a. growth, giving a figure of 136,000 MT of finished products for 1974. In terms of crude steel, this is equivalent to about 194,000 MT.

7.3.1 Demand on the Basis of Import Statistics

Despite the view, expressed in one of the studies reported above, that import statistics are inaccurate, it would seem wrong to dismiss the published statistics out of hand. As developing countries go, Zambia's published statistics are generally taken to be better than average and probably among the best in independent Africa. On the eve of Independence the UN/ECA/FAO Report [56] stressed the need for a sound statistical base for development planning. In response to this, Zambia's published statistics improved a great deal after 1964.

The real issue is to what extent should import statistics form the basis of demand, when the structure of a developing country is rapidly changing. One study, by Maxwell Stamp Associates,[22] on the possibilities of copper fabrication, rejected imports as a basis of demand. But there seems to be little harm in regarding import statistics as complementary to an otherwise independent estimate of demand.

Table 7.6 gives Zambia's imports of iron and steel in value and quantity terms for the periods[23] 1945-53 and 1964-72. The period

Table 7.6: Zambia's Imports[a] of Iron and Steel, 1945-53 and 1964-72

Year	Quantity in Short Tons	Value[b]: Km.[c]
1945	7,750	1.03
1946	5,905	0.93
1947	4,391	0.68
1948	14,549	1.85
1949	27,940	3.20
1950	39,928	4.20
1951	31,652	4.02
1952	53,086	8.81
1953	54,860	9.31
.		
.		
.		
1964	74,070	10.64
1965	107,114	14.71
1966	119,830	16.01
1967	125,280	17.33
1968	158,976	20.84
1969	148,569	20.66
1970	117,066	19.63
1971	227,535	24.84
1972	132,817	17.20
1973[d]	86,990	17.36

a. Includes SITC Divs. 67 + 691 to 694, viz. steel ingots, pig iron, iron and steel bars, rods, plates, strips, rails, wire, pipes, tubes, finished structural parts (iron and steel), containers for storage and transport, wire products (excluding electric), fencing grills, iron gates, nuts and bolts.
b. In current prices, f.o.b.
c. K1 = US $1.55
d. Provisional.

Source: *Annual Statements of External Trade, 1945-53 and 1964-72, Republic of Zambia* [39].

1945-53 has little bearing on current demand. Starting with a low base (probably due to unsatisfied demand during the War), it is not surprising if a high annual rate of growth is registered.[24]

During the ten-year hiatus in the series the economy was generally stagnant. This is, in part, reflected in the 1964-5 steel import figures. If we assume that pent-up war demand was negligible after 1950, then the momentum of the period 1950-53 (a 10 per cent p.a. growth) was clearly lost after 1953. Otherwise the import figure of 1964 or 1965 would be much higher than that shown.

When the imports in terms of quantity over the period 1964 to 1972 are regressed on time[25] (in log-linear form), then imports show an annual growth rate of 8.4 per cent. This growth reflects the massive increase in the output of the construction sector in the first four years of Independence: a staggering 200 per cent increase. And yet even after 1968, imports have remained at a high level.

As long as government continues its policy of extending the social infrastructure to the rural areas and there is a modest mining development, steel requirements could continue to grow at about 8 per cent p.a. However, for the purposes of the computations in the next two chapters, an assumption of a 2 per cent deviation suggests that the range of the rate of growth of demand of 6 per cent p.a. to 10 per cent p.a. is most realistic for Zambia. The computations will therefore be confined to a 6 per cent to 10 per cent range of growth of demand.

If the regression equation is used to predict the level of imports for 1973, one obtains a figure of 199,986 short tons, which is equal to 181,805 MT. This, however, is an estimate of the imports (demand) of finished products. In terms of crude steel, it is equivalent to 259,800 MT.

When comparing the predicted value for 1973 with the estimate, based on 10 months, given in Table 7.6, it is clear that even when the final import figure is obtained, it is unlikely to be as high as the predicted level of imports. One obvious explanation for the discrepancy is the phenomenal price increases during 1972 and 1973 (compare imports by value for 1972 and 1973 in the table), although it is possible that a sizable quantity of steel was lying at the ports serving Zambia (Lobito, Dar es Salaam, Mombasa, Mtwara).[26] There is also evidence which indicates that during 1971 and 1972, there was considerable build-up of inventories when certain Japanese suppliers offered very favourable prices and terms of payment to Zambian steel merchants.

The prediction based on the regression equation is reasonably close to the Mindeco study surveyed above. However, in view of the controversy that was created in Zambia, yet another independent estimate of the demand for iron and steel in Zambia was carried out by the writer.[27]

The findings of this sample survey are summarised below:

ISIC Group No.		MT
230	Metal ore mining	16,000
381	Fabricated metal products	122,718
382	Machinery (non-electric)	6,000
383	Electrical equipment	6,642
384	Transport equipment	38,057
410	Electricity, gas and steam	6,200
400	Construction	38,940
GROSS DEMAND:		234,557
Less inter-industry sales		52,000
NET DEMAND IN 1973:		182,557

A figure of 180,000 MT is taken as the level of demand in 1973, and the range of the rate of growth of demand, 6 per cent to 10 per cent. This will form the basic information on demand for the computations that follow in the next two chapters.

Appendix: The Regression Equation

The imports of steel (SITC Div. 67 only) into Zambia in short tons during 1964-72 were regressed to estimate the annual rate of growth of demand. In order to eliminate annual fluctuation due to transportation problems, etc., a two-year moving average of the imports was used.

The equation fitted was:

$$Y = Ae^{bX}$$

where Y = imports of steel in short tons
X = time.

The result obtained in index form (i.e., 1964 imports = 100) was:

$$Y = 121.51 \, e^{0.08411X} \quad . \quad (R^2 = 0.85260)$$

The standard error of b was 0.01428.

The equation shows that the annual rate of growth of imports over the period 1964 to 1972 was 8.411 per cent. One can say (with 95 per cent confidence) that the true rate lies between 5.6 per cent and 11.2 per cent.

The equation was also used to predict the level of imports for 1973. The result was $Y = 199,986$ short tons, or 181,805 MT.

Notes

1. See Chilton [63], Pratten, Dean and Silberston [76] for the empirical evidence.
2. A cursory correlation of the export price series and data on investment cycles in steel suggests that export prices fell whenever there was excess capacity in the ECSC.
3. IBRD, *Price Forecasts for Major Primary Commodities,* IBRD/IDA, June 1974, report no. 467 (mimeo).
4. Unfortunately all Zambian import statistics are published *f.o.b. only*, and not c.i.f.
5. According to SERIECO Report [54], Vol. 2, p. 105.
6. According to a steel merchant in Zambia, the inland transport cost−over 1200 miles−is $42 per MT. The Zambian border is roughly 600 miles from the port.
7. The equipment was made up of tanks, reaction vessels, kilns, etc.
8. See Cockerill and Silberston [64], p. 83.
9. C. Pratten, R.M. Dean and A. Silberston [76], p. 74.
10. R.S. Barnes [61] reports (in 1974) that the largest electric arc furnace has a capacity of 100 MT per working hour.
11. Direct reduction does not remove any silica, sulphur, etc., present in the ore.
12. Uniform size of pellets promotes a better distribution of gas, and therefore savings in gas consumption.
13. This depends on the type of hydrocarbon, e.g., LNG, LPG, Naphtha.
14. The highest degree of metallisation is not *necessarily* the best for steel production.
15. Zambian Steel Project Development Report, Bechtel International Corporation, San Francisco, April 1971 [41].
16. At that time the world export price of steel was only just beginning to recover from the drastic slump of the mid-sixties.
17. Unfortunately I was unable to trace this study and therefore cannot comment on its reliability.
18. Stands for Industrial Development Corporation of Zambia, wholly owned by the State.
19. Mindeco stands for Mining and Industrial Development Corporation, which is wholly owned by the State.
20. It was at this point that Energoprojekt asked the present writer for a report on the demand for steel in Zambia.
21. These 18 companies included all the major companies.
22. Maxwell Stamp Associates, Pre-investment Study of the Copper Fabricating Industry in the East and Central African Sub-region, London, 1969 [49].
23. In the intervening period what is now Zambia was part of a customs union with S. Rhodesia and what is now Malawi. No separate import statistics are available for this period.
24. For what it is worth, the rate was, in fact, 35 per cent p.a.

25. The regression equation is shown in the Appendix to this chapter.
26. Press reports in 1975 in Zambia indicated that some steel destined for Zambia was rusting in the open air at Dar es Salaam for over two years! And this was due to the failure of the Tanzanian Customs authority in clearing the good for removal to Zambia.
27. Details of this demand survey can be found in the writer's doctoral dissertation, Oxford, 1975. See Dore [13].

8 COMPUTATIONAL RESULTS OF THE MODEL

In this chapter, the main results of the computations of the model developed in the preceding pages are given. Section 8.1 of this chapter summarises the range of parameter values considered relevant for the computation. Sections 8.2 and 8.3 are devoted to the presentation of the results of the computations.

8.1 The Range of Parameter Values

Chapter 7 discussed economies of scale in direct reduction steel-making processes. It was found that there is some uncertainty as to an accurate estimate of the economies of scale parameter α for DR-EF processes. However, the empirical evidence reviewed in that chapter points very strongly to α being close to 0.6, as indeed the 'six-tenth rule' suggests. Thus all computations will be confined to $\alpha = 0.6$.

Next consider the demand growth rate β. It was shown in Chapter 7 that:
- (a) demand in 1973 was around 180,000 MT;
- (b) that in the past (1964-72) imports of iron and steel have grown at a proportionate rate of 8.4 per cent p.a.

This rate of growth of demand was considered high and was more reflective of:
- (a) low initial base;
- (b) improving quality of statistics collected by the Zambian Central Statistical Office;
- (c) high government spending in a newly-independent republic on health, housing and education.

In the near future, therefore, the rate of growth of steel imports can be expected to be lower than 8.4 per cent. But the domestic availability of steel—if and when the plant is built—could lead to some induced demand. For these reasons, the range of the rate of growth of demand of between 6 per cent p.a. and 10 per cent p.a. should be adequate.

The treatment of *price relatives* is a little more complex and deserves some detailed consideration.

Referring to equation (4.1) or (4.27), it can be seen that the integral is a sum of three cost components, all valued in terms of foreign exchange:

u(i)	(investment)
[d(i) − r(i)] m(i)	(imports)
br(i)m(i) + G·c(i)x(i)	(production costs)

The purchasing power of foreign exchange is falling and the rate of increase of OECD export prices—for the period 1966 to 1973—can be considered one measure of this fall. Let this rate be σ_0, $0 < \sigma_0 < 1$.

Now, if all three cost components rise at the same rate, then the optimal policy will be unaffected. Now suppose that the first component, investment, rises at the rate σ_1, and the second at the rate σ_2. Then, assuming domestic costs do not change, we have

$$u(i)e^{(\sigma_1 - \sigma_0)i}$$

$$[d(i) - r(i)] \, m(i)e^{(\sigma_2 - \sigma_0)i}$$
$$br(i) + G·c(i)x(i)$$

It was found[1] that σ_1 was not significantly different from σ_0, i.e., that the rate of increase of OECD investment goods' prices was not significantly different from the general rate of increase of OECD exports taken as a whole. For this reason no adjustment of u(i) is necessary, as $e^{(\sigma_1 - \sigma_0)i}$ is taken as 1. As for the IBRD data, their forecast in the export price inflation is largely based on machinery and equipment which are, in fact, investment goods and so again, no adjustment is necessary.

It was also shown in Chapter 7 that

(i) if the OECD data on export price inflation is used, then $(\sigma_2 - \sigma_0) = -0.02$ or -0.03.

(ii) if the IBRD forecasts are used, together with a small adverse terms of trade effect, then the estimate of the real change in the price of steel of -0.02 becomes -0.005.

The computations therefore fall into two main categories. In the first category it is assumed that Zambia's ability to earn foreign exchange is unchanged, i.e., the real import price of steel will continue to fall at 2 per cent or 3 per cent p.a. In the second category, the IBRD forecast in the fall of the real price of steel (viz. 2 per cent p.a.) is adjusted by the IBRD forecast in the fall of the real price of copper (viz. 1.5 per cent), Zambia's main foreign exchange earner.

The final component is domestic cost of production. One would really need to disaggregate all inputs used in the production of steel and compare the rates of price increases of these inputs with the general rate σ_0.[2] In the absence of evidence, it has been necessary to assume in Section 8.2 that the domestic cost of production will rise at the same rate[3] as the general rate σ_0. (Since there is now only one value of σ, viz. the rate of increase/fall in the price of imports, the subscript of σ is omitted from here onwards.) This simple set of assumptions regarding price relatives will be called *Model One* and the computational results are set out in Section 8.2. In Section 8.3, technological progress is introduced into the model and is called *Model Two*. In Model Two, domestic costs of production fall at the same rate as import prices. It will be seen that the computed results of Sections 8.2 and 8.3 present some interesting contrasts.

Since Dynamic Programming solutions are sensitive to initial conditions, it seemed essential to vary both the initial demand (a_1) and initial import price (a_2). These computations will, in turn, suggest important conclusions about the timing and scale of plants.

Finally, for the two pairs $\beta = 6$ per cent and $\sigma = -3$ per cent, and $\beta = 6$ per cent with $\sigma = -0.005$, some sensitivity to the costs of production is reported. This is important in view of the approximate nature of the data on costs of production. Chart 2 summarises the main ranges of parameter variation.

Before the numerical results are considered, it is necessary to make a few general observations. It should be noted that the standard functional relation of DP is a discrete approximation of Bellman's equation, which is a partial differential equation for which no general analytic solution exists. Secondly, numerical accuracy depends on the grid size—the finer the grid the better the approximation. The finer the grid the larger the computer store or memory required—the basic drawback of Dynamic Programming (Bellman has dubbed it 'the curse of dimensionality'). However, with one state variable and one decision variable, storage is not a problem provided (a) one is prepared to accept a finite horizon and some (finite) grid, and (b) optimal solutions are interpreted as lying between the grid points. As pointed out in Chapter 5, this means that the 'true' value of the optimal capacity at time i is $x^*(i) \pm \Delta$. When $\Delta = 10$, we get reasonably acceptable solutions. For the problem on hand, storage requirements grow exponentially:

(a) the longer the horizon;

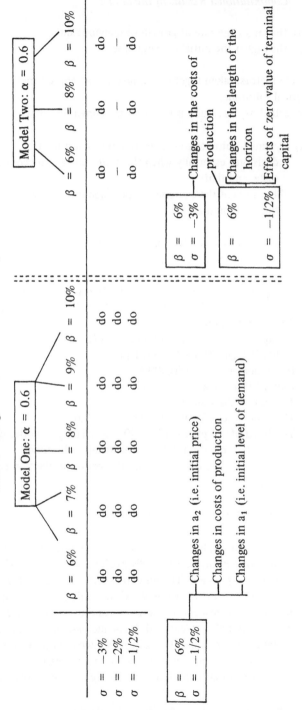

Chart 2: Range of Parameters used in Computations

	Model One: α = 0.6					
	β = 6%	β = 7%	β = 8%	β = 9%	β = 10%	
σ = −3%	do	do	do	do	do	Changes in a_2 (i.e. initial price)
σ = −2%	do	do	do	do	do	Changes in costs of production
σ = −1/2%	do	do	do	do	do	Changes in a_1 (i.e. initial level of demand)

β = 6%
σ = −1/2%

	Model Two: α = 0.6			
	β = 6%	β = 8%	β = 10%	
	do	do	do	
	−	−	−	
	do	do	do	

β = 6%
σ = −3% ──── Changes in the costs of production

β = 6%
σ = −1/2% ┌── Changes in the length of the horizon
           └── Effects of zero value of terminal capital

(b) the larger the rate of growth of demand; and

(c) the higher the initial demand base.

All these factors, taken together, emphasise the approximate nature of numerical solutions.

Nevertheless, this study is based on the conviction that:

(a) dynamic optimisation leads to better investment
decisions, especially when there are substantial economies of scale, and that

(b) the results of the exercise can be made intuitively appealing to the decision maker.

The computational results[4] that follow are based on some constant parameters. These are as follows:

1. Except when stated, the horizon is 20 years. In Section 8.3 some sensitivity to changes in the length of the horizon is reported.

2. The minimum investment $\bar{u} = \$90m$, which leads to a (minimum) capacity of $\bar{x}$, set at 200,000 MT. (The source is ENERGOPROJEKT Report [43].)

3. Initial demand $a_1 = 180,000$ MT.

4. Initial CIF price $a_2 = \$300/MT$.

5. The rate of discount $\lambda = 10\%$.

6. The economies of scale parameter $\alpha = 0.60$.

7. The fixed life of plants, $T' = 30$ years. The productive capacity of a plant does not deteriorate during its lifetime.

8. It will be recalled that the domestic cost of production equation was:

$$C(i) = br(i)m(i) + G \cdot c(i)x(i)   . \tag{4.35}$$

In this equation, b is approximated by the ratio of labour to non-labour costs in the ENERGOPROJEKT Report [43]. b has the value of 8.4 per cent. The unit costs $c(i)$, were taken from Miller [69], and G is the factor by which the unit costs are multiplied in order to correspond to Zambian conditions. In general, it is assumed that G is at least 2.0. If the increase in gas and oil prices are taken into account, $G = 2.7$. As shown later in Section 8.3, $c(i)$ fall at the same rate as the fall in import prices.

9. It is assumed that there is a one-year lag between investment and

capacity creation.

8.2 Results of Model One

Table 8.1 summarises the computational results when $\sigma = -3\%$ for different rates of growth of demand. Table 8.2 corresponds to the case when $\sigma = -2\%$.

The results show that *if the production cost level can be considered realistic for Zambia*, then the optimal timing for the first plant is now. Its scale varies with the demand growth rate β, but the range β under consideration gives a range of between 220,000 MT and 240,000 MT. The number of years' backlogging refers to the number of years between plants during which the 'excess' demand is satisfied by importing. The significance of the results is best seen graphically, as in Figs. 8.1 to 8.5. It will be seen that there is some excess capacity in the first plant: if demand grows at 6 per cent, then there is 22 per cent excess capacity *initially*, which is wiped out within three years. Over the next 11 years, in this case, 'excess' demand is satisfied ('backlogged') by importing and in year 15, the second plant is initiated—which comes on stream in the year 16.

With the increase in β, backlogging falls and the second plant is brought forward in time. Also, the greater the β, the greater the size of the second plant.

Furthermore, as σ is increased, i.e., from -3% to -2%, backlogging falls and the second plant is built sooner, as would be expected since future imports are more costly now.

It would be best to consider all sensitivity in the costs of production together later in this section. One may perhaps anticipate those results and simply state here that when import costs are falling rather rapidly, it is quite possible to find that the optimal thing to do is to invest now—or never, depending on the costs of production.

Consider now the second category of data, namely the IBRD data. As mentioned before, according to IBRD forecasts, $\sigma = -0.005$. Furthermore, if the recent increases in the price of oil and gas are taken into account, then the factor G is at least 2.7. (Lower values of G are investigated below where sensitivity in the costs of production is considered.) Table 8.3 summarises the optimal timing and scale of plants for $\beta = 6\%$ to $\beta = 10\%$.

The table shows that with a higher level of costs of production, the optimal timing of the first plant is year 7, assuming demand grows at 6 per cent per annum, and even if the demand growth rate is as high as 10 per cent — which is most unlikely, as stated above — it is still

Table 8.1: Model One: Main Results: $G = 2.0$, $\sigma = -3\%$[c]

β	PLANT 1				PLANT 2				PLANT 3				PLANT 4				f^{*}[b] (US $m)
	Invest. $m	t^*_1[a]	Scale '000MT	No. of Years' Back-Logging	Invest. $m	t^*_2	Scale '000MT	No. of Years' Back-Logging	Invest. $m	t^*_3	Scale '000MT	No. of Years' Back-Logging	Invest. $m	t^*_4	Scale '000MT	No. of Years' Back-Logging	
6%	95.3	1	220	11	114.8	15	300			—				—			490.97
7%	95.3	1	220	11	138.5	14	410			—				—			520.22
8%	97.9	1	230	10	157.8	14	510			—				—			538.14
9%	100.4	1	240	9	161.5	13	530		90.0	17	200	0		—			524.29
10%	100.4	1	240	6	136.4	9	400		110.2	14	280	1	90.0	17	200	0	639.77

a. t^* refers to the optimal timing of investment, e.g. year 1, year 15 etc.

b. f^{*} is the optimised value of the objective functional.

c. All other parameters as given in Section 8.1.

Table 8.2: Model One: Main Results: G = 2.0, $\sigma = -3\%$[c]

	PLANT 1			PLANT 2				PLANT 3				PLANT 4				f*[b]
β	t^*_1[a]	Invest. Scale $ m	'000MT	No. of Years' Back-Logging	t^*_2	Invest. Scale $ m	'000MT	No. of Years' Back-Logging	t^*_3	Invest. Scale $ m	'000MT	No. of Years' Back-Logging	t^*_4	Invest. Scale $ m	'000MT	US $ m
6%	1	95.3	220	10	14	112.5	290			—						480.89
7%	1	95.3	220	8	11	128.1	360			—						558.98
8%	1	97.9	230	6	11	128.1	360	1	16	90.0	200			—		519.88
9%	1	97.9	230	5	8	128.1	360	0	13	90.0	200	2	19	90.0	200	326.36
10%	1	100.4	240	5	8	134.4	390	0	13	95.3	220	0	16	90.0	200	633.64

a. t^* refers to the optimal timing of investment.
b. f^* is the optimised value of the objective functional.
c. All other parameters as given in Section 8.1.

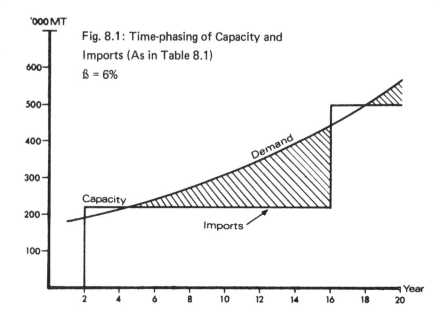

Fig. 8.1: Time-phasing of Capacity and Imports (As in Table 8.1)

ß = 6%

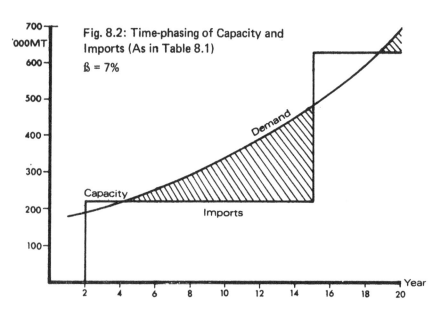

Fig. 8.2: Time-phasing of Capacity and Imports (As in Table 8.1)

ß = 7%

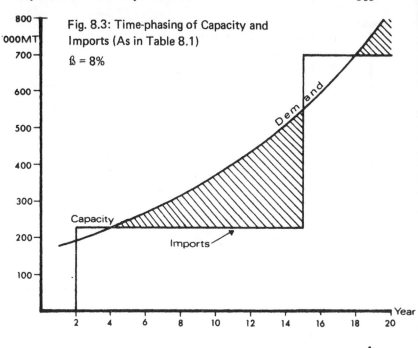

Fig. 8.3: Time-phasing of Capacity and Imports (As in Table 8.1)

ß = 8%

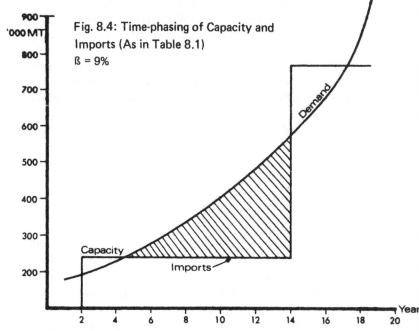

Fig. 8.4: Time-phasing of Capacity and Imports (As in Table 8.1)

ß = 9%

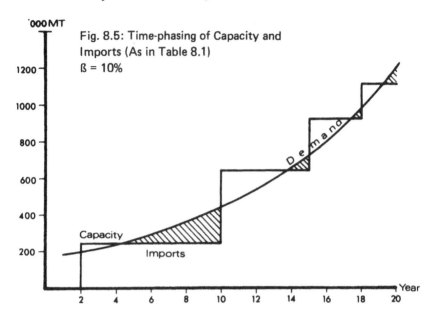

Fig. 8.5: Time-phasing of Capacity and Imports (As in Table 8.1) ß = 10%

optimal to delay the first plant for five years.

If 6 per cent growth in demand is more realistic for Zambia for the medium term, then taking the demand and price base year as 1973, the first plant must come on stream in the year 1981.[5] Obviously this result depends on the level of costs of production used here. But it must be emphasised that the costs can by no means be regarded as being overestimated. Taking equation (4.35), with b = 0.084 and G = 2.7 and dividing the total costs by the size of the first plant yields an *average* unit cost figure of \$223.68/MT.[6]

The timing and scale of the second plant in Table 8.3 requires little comment. The results are broadly parallel with the earlier results given in this section. Perhaps it is worth restating that when demand exceeds the capacity of the first plant, there is an optimal 'waiting time' before a second plant is built so that the benefits of economies of scale on a larger plant are obtained. The results are shown graphically in Figs. 8.6 to 8.10.

In the results presented so far a somewhat odd phenomenon will have been noticed: when $\beta \geqslant 9\%$, the size of the third and fourth plants declines. This is due to the combined affect of the terminal conditions as well as the treatment of terminal capital and is discussed later. But since this only happens towards the end of the horizon from the point of view of *current* decision-making, this is not significant.

Table 8.3: Model One: Main Results: G = 2.7, $\sigma = -0.005$[c]

β	PLANT 1 t*_1 [a]	PLANT 1 No. of Years' Back-Logging	PLANT 1 Invest. Scale $ m	PLANT 1 '000MT	PLANT 2 t*_2	PLANT 2 No. of Years' Back-Logging	PLANT 2 Invest. Scale $ m	PLANT 2 '000MT	PLANT 3 t*_3	PLANT 3 No. of Years' Back-Logging	PLANT 3 Invest. Scale $ m	PLANT 3 '000MT	PLANT 4 t*_4	PLANT 4 No. of Years' Back-Logging	PLANT 4 Invest. Scale $ m	PLANT 4 '000MT	PLANT 4 f*[b] US $ m
6%	7	5	112.5	290	13		92.7	210			—				—		589.01
7%	6	5	112.5	290	12		119.3	320			—				—		629.76
8%	6	5	117.1	310	12		125.9	350			—				—		666.11
9%	5	4	117.1	310	11		128.1	360	15	0	90.0	200			—		718.86
10%	5	4	121.5	330	11		136.4	400	15	0	90.0	200	17	0	90.0	200	720.97

a. t* refers to optimal timing of investment.
b. f* is the optimised value of the objective functional.
c. All other parameters as given in Section 8.1.

The sensitivity to costs of production is discussed next, for both categories of data, viz. the OECD data and the IBRD data.

8.2.1 Sensitivity in the Costs of Production

Consider first the case where $\sigma = -3\%$. Table 8.4 sets out the effect on optimal policy of varying the level of domestic production costs by considering different values of G. The table shows a sharp discontinuity when G is increased from 2.1 to 2.2. It also follows immediately that if the rate of fall of import prices is 3% and the appropriate cost level given by G is 2.7 (as stated earlier), then the optimal policy is to delay investment till the year 19. The practical impact of such a policy is to rely on imports throughout which emerges as the optimal policy. This sharp discontinuity needs to be explained.

Recall the static make-or-buy framework discussed in Chapter 3 and illustrated in Fig. 3.2 (p.24). Now if the quantity demanded is a function of time, the same diagram can be drawn with time instead of quantity on the horizontal axis (Fig. 8.11). The diagram shows that a sufficient condition for not investing now is that the unit cost of imports be less than the unit cost of domestic production. However, if there are economies of scale in domestic production, so that the unit cost of production falls with time (as demand increases), then there will come a time when domestic cost of production per unit will be

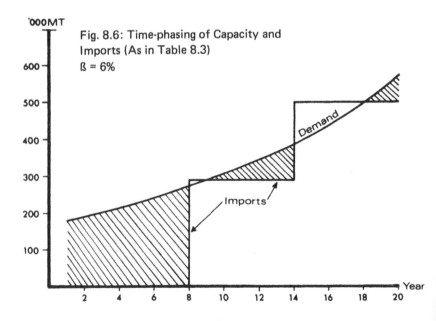

Fig. 8.6: Time-phasing of Capacity and Imports (As in Table 8.3)

ß = 6%

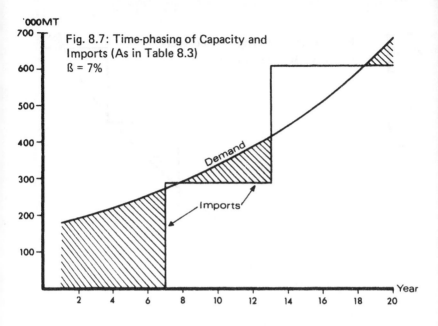

Fig. 8.7: Time-phasing of Capacity and Imports (As in Table 8.3)
ß = 7%

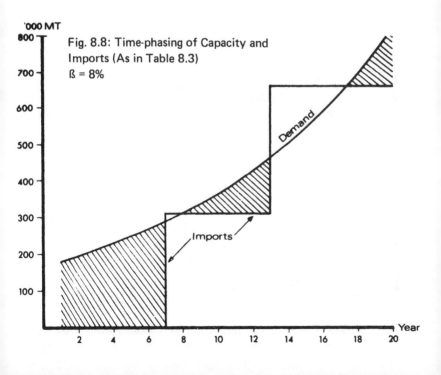

Fig. 8.8: Time-phasing of Capacity and Imports (As in Table 8.3)
ß = 8%

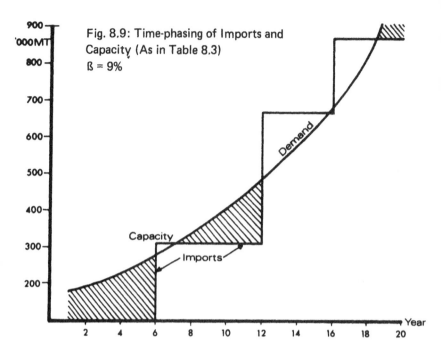

Fig. 8.9: Time-phasing of Imports and Capacity (As in Table 8.3)
ß = 9%

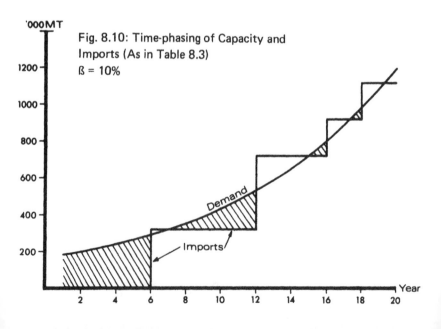

Fig. 8.10: Time-phasing of Capacity and Imports (As in Table 8.3)
ß = 10%

Table 8.4: Mode One: Sensitivity to Changes in Costs of Production[a]
$\beta = 6\%$, $\sigma = -3\%$

G	t_1 *[b]	PLANT 1 Scale ('000MT)	t_2 *	PLANT 2 Scale ('000MT)	f^* (US $ m)
1.0	1	260	14	200	335.84
1.5	1	240	14	220	428.86
2.0	1	220	15	260	501.96
2.1	1	210	15	320	508.51
2.2	19	560		—	5.92
2.25	19	560		—	6.54
2.5	19	560		—	78.10
2.7	19	560		—	241.03

a. All other paramerers as given in Section 8.1.
b. As before t* refers to optimal timing.

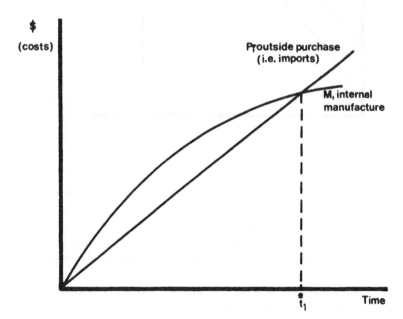

Fig. 8.11

below import cost and the first plant should come on stream at time $t*_1$. This is of course based on the assumption that unit import cost is *constant* throughout the period.

However, the results in Table 8.4 are based on the assumption that import prices are *falling* at 3 per cent p.a. Therefore, informally speaking, the timing of the first plant will depend on the relative 'curvatures' of the P and M curves of Fig. 8.11. Indeed, it is quite possible for one of the curves to be entirely above or entirely below the other, throughout the horizon, with no intersection. This is illustrated

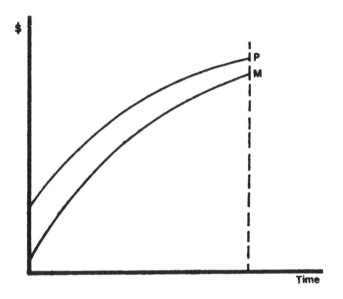

Fig. 8.12

in Fig. 8.12. Under these circumstances, optimal timing of the first plant is either now or never, depending on whether P or M is initially higher. Fig. 8.12 illustrates the case where P, outside purchase, is higher initially, and so the optimal timing of the first plant is now.[7]

In formal terms, the optimal timing of the first plant depends on:

(a) the initial levels of P and M; and
(b) the rates of change of P and M with respect to time.

This explains the 'knife edge' characteristic of the model in the results contained in Table 8.4. To be sure, this characteristic is a consequence of an asymmetry in the model: import prices are allowed to fall over time because of the expected and observed efficiency gains in the production of steel. However, no corresponding efficiency gain parameter appears in the domestic cost of production: see equation (4.35). In Section 8.3 such an efficiency gain in domestic production cost is introduced and, as is shown there, the knife edge characteristic disappears.

Now consider the second category of data, namely those based on the IBRD forecasts. Here $\sigma = -0.005$. This produces a modest, but not insignificant, fall in the import price.[8]

Table 8.5 sets out the effect on optimal policy of varying the level of domestic costs of production by considering different values of G.

Table 8.5: Model One: Sensitivity to Changes in the Cost of Production[a]

$\beta = 6\%$, $\sigma = -0.005$

G	PLANT 1 t^*_1 [b]	PLANT 1 Scale ('000MT)	PLANT 2 t^*_2	PLANT 2 Scale ('000MT)
2.4	1	220	12	270
2.5	3	230	12	260
2.6	5	260	13	240
2.7	7	290	13	210
2.9	13	310	18	200
3.0	14	320	19	200
3.2	19	560	—	—

a. All other parameters as given in Section 8.1.
b. t* refers to optimal timing of plants.

The results show that while there is no knife edge as in the previous table, the timing and scale of plants are both functions of the level of domestic costs of production. As mentioned before, the value of G of 2.7 seems to be the likely level of costs for Zambian conditions; it may be even higher, but it seems unlikely to be less than that.To justify immediate investment (for a plant of capacity 220,000 MT), *average* unit costs of production have to be about $212.8 per MT or less.

8.2.2 Sensitivity to Changes in Initial Import Price

All the results presented above were based on an initial import price of $300/MT. It is now necessary to consider changes in the initial import price. This is essential for two reasons. First, it was shown in Chapter 7 that the export price of steel has exhibited a cyclical pattern. Second, since one anyway expects optimal solutions to be sensitive to initial conditions, it is essential to display this, if only to inject a degree of caution for actual decision-making. Table 8.6 shows that even a $5 difference delays the first plant by a year. Thus the base price has to be estimated with some care, to represent an approximation to an 'equilibrium world price'.

Lastly, it is quite possible to make an error in the initial demand and Table 8.7 gives the effect on optimal policy of a range of initial demand levels. In all the results given before Table 8.7, it was assumed that the initial level of demand was 180,000 MT (in the year 1973). The table shows that in order to justify immediate investment, demand would have to be at least 28 per cent above the 1973 estimate, i.e., 230,000 MT. Alternatively, it implies that the excess of production over domestic demand can be readily exported until domestic demand catches up with capacity — a sort of 'negative backlogging'.

Table 8.6: Model One: Sensitivity in Initial Price[a]
β = 6%, σ = −0.005, G = 2.7

Initial Price $/MT	PLANT 1 t^*_1 [b]	PLANT 1 Scale ('000MT)	PLANT 2 t^*_2	PLANT 2 Scale ('000MT)
300	7	290	13	210
295	8	300	13	200
290	9	310	14	200
285	13	310	18	200
280	14	320	19	200
250	19	560	—	—

a. All other parameters as given in Section 8.1.
b. t* refers to optimal timing.

Before passing on to Model Two in the next section, it is perhaps worth restating the major results of this section. Firstly, optimal solutions are very sensitive to differences in the rates of change of price and costs of production. The use of $\sigma = -3\%$ or -2% produces a knife edge: depending on the costs it is optimal to invest immediately and, if not, to rely exclusively on imports. This is due to the fact that while import price is explicitly a declining function of time, costs of production have to be as low as $177 per MT to justify immediate investment.

Table 8.7: Model One: Sensitivity to Initial Demand[a]
$\beta = 6\%$, $\sigma = -0.005$, G = 2.7

| Initial Demand ('000MT) | PLANT 1 | | PLANT 2 | |
	t^*_1[b]	Scale ('000MT)	t^*_2	Scale ('000MT)
150	13	210	18	200
160	7	250	14	200
180	7	290	13	210
200	4	270	12	280
220	3	280	11	330
230	1	260	10	350
240	1	270	10	360

a. All other parameters are as given in Section 8.1.
b. t^* refers to the optimal timing of plants.

When the rate of decline of import price is only moderate, i.e., $\sigma = -0.005$, average unit costs of production should be of the order of $223 per MT in order to justify a first plant with a capacity of 290,000 MT to come on stream in the year 8 (see Fig. 8.6). The full demand growth range of $\beta = 6\%$ to $\beta = 10\%$ does not increase the size of the first plant by more than 14 per cent and the highest value of β only brings it forward by two years. As the figures show there is a one year excess capacity for $\beta \leqslant 8\%$, which rises to two years for $\beta = 9\%$ or 10%.

The scale of the second plant shows a much greater range, from 210,000 MT to 400,000 MT, but the backlogging time between the two plants is at least four years. So while the scale of the second plant is sensitive to demand growth, its timing is not too sensitive.

Finally, the optimal solutions are clearly a function of the horizon. In the next section some sensitivity in the length of the horizon in the case of Model Two is considered.

8.3 Results of Model Two

As stated in Chapter 4, Model Two differs from Model One in that in the former:

(a) capital-saving technological progress is introduced, so that capital requirements per unit of output fall through time, and
(b) an efficiency gains parameter is introduced into domestic costs.

The first requires evidence of efficiency gains in the production of capital goods required for iron and steel-making – mining machinery, pelletisation units, reduction vessels, electric arc furnaces and continuous casting machines. It is entirely possible that the production of these capital goods is itself subject to economies of scale and without a great deal of empirical data it would be quite difficult to separate efficiency gains and the effects of scale. Nevertheless, from the point of view of the purchaser of steel-making plants, some 'gains' through time are entirely feasible either because more plants are demanded leading to economies of scale or because the producers are able to use the required inputs more efficiently. In the absence of direct evidence, it has been assumed that capital costs will fall at the same rate as the rate of fall of the import price of steel.

Again, with regard to efficiency gains in the domestic production of steel, there is no direct evidence, since the steel industry does not yet exist in Zambia. However, throughout the planning exercise domestic output is valued at world prices, and if the projected industry is to be competitive, i.e., replace imports, then efficiency gains in domestic production must at least equal the real fall in the price of imports.

It is almost certain that because of technological progress the size of the largest plant continues to increase over time. This would not affect the current exercise in any way for demand is used as a constraint which means that the largest plant size is not an effective constraint. But it is also true that because of technological progress the minimum plant size, for the same technology, often rises too. This has certainly happened to the BF-BOS process for steel-making. However, this possible complication has been ignored: it is assumed that the minimum plant available throughout the horizon is the same, viz. 200,000 MT.

Table 8.8 and 8.9 give the optimal investment plans when $\sigma = -3\%$ and $-1/2\%$ respectively. When $\sigma = -3\%$, the optimal timing of the first plant is between year 6 and year 8, depending on demand growth and its range is 310,000 to 360,000 MT. The timing of the second plant is between year 11 and year 15, the former being for a 10% growth in demand and the latter for a 6% growth in demand. The range of the second plant is much larger than the first; it is in fact between 210,000 MT and 370,000 MT.

When $\sigma = -1/2\%$ (Table 8.9), the first plant should be built sooner, in year 5 or year 6. Its range is 270,000 MT to 330,000 MT. The second plant, too, should be built sooner, between year 10 and year 13 and its range is 230,000 MT to 350,000 MT.

It is immediately clear that when domestic cost also falls at the same rate as the import price, the knife edge (observed in the results of Model One when $\sigma = -3\%$) disappears, though *the faster the rate of decline of import price, the later the investments should be made.* The non-existence of the knife edge is further confirmed in the sensitivity to changes in the domestic costs of production given in Table 8.10.

Table 8.10 shows, once again, that on the basis of the parameters estimated in Chapters 6 and 7 of this book and the assumptions underlying the model, there does not seem to be a case for immediate investment in steel production in Zambia. To justify immediate investment for a plant of 210,000 MT, average unit costs of production have to be as low as $198 per MT.

Next, Figs. 8.13 to 8.15 show the phasing of capacity in relation to demand for the results in Table 8.8. While these diagrams also show the backlogging of imports, Table 8.11 shows the backlogged imports between the first two plants in greater detail.

8.3.1 Terminal Constraints and the Length of the Horizon

As mentioned before, the dynamic optimisation of a non-convex problem was made computable by taking demand as a datum. This, in turn, puts an upper bound on the state space, by virtue of the fact that the horizon is finite. It therefore follows that the optimal policy *as a whole* is dependent on the length of the horizon and the value of terminal capital. This gives rise to two important questions:

1. Does the optimal policy, dependent as it is on terminal conditions, make good 'planning sense' and is it operationally useful?
2. What bearing does the optimal policy have on *current* investment planning problems?

Table 8.8: Model Two: Main Results: G = 2.7, $\sigma = -3\%$[b]

	PLANT 1			No. of Years' Back-Logging	PLANT 2			No. of Years' Back-Logging	PLANT 3			No. of Years' Back-Logging	PLANT 4			
β	t^*_1 [a]	Invest. Scale $ m	Scale '000MT		t^*_2	Invest. Scale $ m	Scale '000MT		t^*_3	Invest. Scale $ m	Scale '000MT		t^*_4	Invest. Scale $ m	Scale '000MT	f^{*c} US $ m
6%	8	94.9	310	5	15	60.9	210			—				—		518.90
8%	7	103.4	340	5	13	89.3	360			—				—		594.29
10%	6	110.2	360	4	11	96.4	370	0	15	59.1	200	0	17	56.4	200	647.94

a. t^* refers to optimal timing of investment.
b. All other parameters as given in Section 8.1.
c. f^* is the optimised value of the objective functional.

Table 8.9: Model Two: Main Results G:= 2.7, $\sigma = -0.005$[c]

β	PLANT 1				PLANT 2				PLANT 3				PLANT 4				
	t^*_1[a]	Invest. Scale $ m	Scale '000MT	No. of Years' Back-Logging	t^*_2	Invest. Scale $ m	Scale '000MT	No. of Years' Back-Logging	t^*_3	Invest. Scale $ m	Scale '000MT	No. of Years' Back-Logging	t^*_4	Invest. Scale $ m	Scale '000MT	No. of Years' Back-Logging	f^*[b] US $ m
6%	6	105.1	270	6	13	92.1	230	3		—				—			571.49
8%	5	110.2	290	5	11	115.6	330	5	19	82.3	200	3		—			311.46
10%	5	119.1	330	3	10	120.4	350	3	14	84.7	200	0	17	83.6	200	0	708.98

a. t^* refers to optimal timing of investment.
b. f^* is the optimised value of the objective functional.
c. All other parameters as given in Section 8.1.

Table 8.10: Model Two: Sensitivity in the Costs of Production[a]
$\beta = 6\%$, $\sigma = -3\%$

G	PLANT 1		PLANT 2	
		Scale		Scale
	t^*_1 [b]	('000MT)	t^*_2	('000MT)
2.2	1	210	9	290
2.5	5	260	14	250
2.7	8	310	15	210
3.0	15	330	—	—

a. All other parameters as given in Section 8.1.
b. t^* refers to optimal timing

Table 8.11: Model Two: Backlogged Imports Between the First Two Plants in Table 8.8

β	Volume in MT	Present Value, in $m
6%	305,653	$ 17.76
8%	315,829	22.82
10%	255,093	22.88

An attempt will be made to answer these questions after some further results are presented. These results concern the valuation of terminal capital and the length of the horizon.

Table 8.12 contains a sample of results which show both the sensitivity to the length of the horizon and the effect of arbitrarily putting the value of terminal capital to zero. The results bring out the following features. Firstly, optimal policies are obviously a function of the length of the horizon, but approximately the first half of the horizon has a reasonably close policy with respect to timing and scale. More specifically, the timing and scale of the first plant is almost identical: it should be built in year 6 or year 7 and its capacity should be between 270,000-280,000 MT. The timing of the second plant should be between years 13 and 15, though the range of the second plant is larger.

Secondly, zero terminal valuation largely affects the 'last' plant in

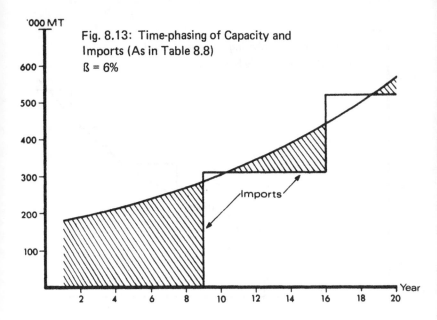

Fig. 8.13: Time-phasing of Capacity and Imports (As in Table 8.8)
ß = 6%

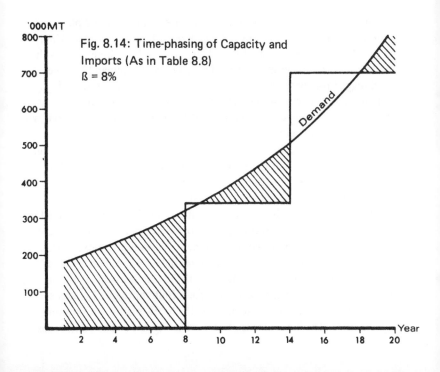

Fig. 8.14: Time-phasing of Capacity and Imports (As in Table 8.8)
ß = 8%

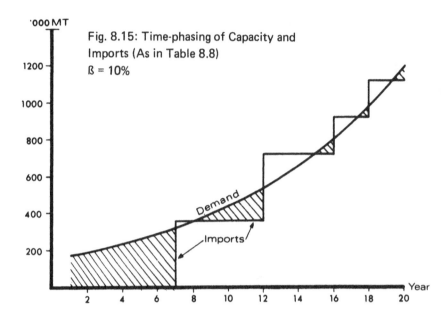

Fig. 8.15: Time-phasing of Capacity and Imports (As in Table 8.8)
ß = 10%

the horizon: with a 20-year horizon and $\beta = 6\%$, the second plant vanishes as a result of putting a zero value on terminal capital. When the horizon is 30 years, the third plant is delayed by three years — the delay of course increases its scale, i.e., after excess demand has been backlogged for three years. However, the results of zero terminal valuation are by way of illustration only; this was an attempt to separate out the differential impacts of the two terminal conditions, viz. the finite horizon and the terminal valuation.

Having presented these results, it is now possible to show some links with the existing literature on optimum growth theory. This will, in turn, help to answer the two questions posed above.

First, it will be helpful to set aside the specific features of the models computed in this book, viz. non-convexities. Second, instead of minimising all costs, as in the models considered here, let the objective functional be the maximisation of some social welfare index, $W(t)$, assumed to be concave and twice differentiable. Then, Mirrlees and Hammond [27] have shown that even if the true horizon, T, is not known, an operationally useful plan for a finite horizon, T_0, exists, provided the welfare loss associated with the T_0 plan is within some agreed limit. The basic idea is illustrated in Fig. 8.16. The continuous

Table 8.12: Mode Two: Sensitivity in the Horizon and Zero Terminal Value
(β = 6%, σ = −½%, G = 2.7, all other parameters as in Section 8.1)

Horizon: Years	PLANT 1				PLANT 2				PLANT 3			
	t^*_1 [a]	Invest. $ m	Scale '000MT	No. of Years' Back-Logging	t^*_2	Invest. $ m	Scale '000MT	No. of Years' Back-Logging	t^*_3	Invest. $ m	Scale '000MT	f^* [b]
Part One: Sensitivity to Changes in the Horizon:												
20	6	105.1	270	6	13	92.1	230			—		571.49
25	6	107.4	280	7	15	117.4	350			—		673.93
30	6	107.4	280	7	15	123.3	380	0	22	81.0	200	730.73
Part Two: Effect of Putting Zero Terminal Value:												
20	7	113.6	310			—						711.17
30	6	109.7	290	7	15	121.4	370	3	25	113.5	360	885.32

a. t refers to optimal timing of plants.
b. f is the optimised value of the objective functional.

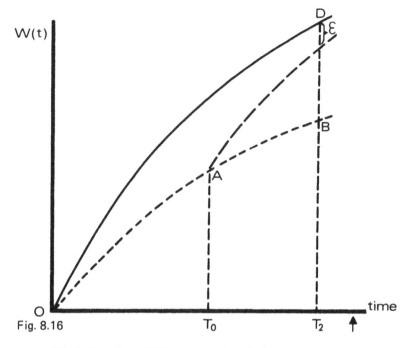

Fig. 8.16

curve, OD, is the value of W(t) associated with the true but unknown horizon, $T > T_1 > T_0$. Then the operationally useful plans, OA and AG, form an 'agreeable plan' if the (small) welfare loss of DG is less than the maximum acceptable welfare loss, ϵ, i.e., if DG $< \epsilon$.

However, the existence of agreeable plans is proved with two crucial assumptions, viz.

(i) the objective functional is strictly concave,
(ii) the production function is concave, i.e., there are no economies of scale.

But, as has been repeatedly maintained, the non-convexities of the models computed here are their most essential characteristics. Consequently, no numerical value can be placed on ϵ for that purpose and so the optimal policies, or plans, computed here fail to conform to the strict definition of an agreeable plan, as given by Hammond and Mirrlees.

But surely the gravamen of 'Agreeable Plans' is how restrictive is the choice of a finite horizon on current decisions, and what is the social welfare loss of artificially decomposing an infinite horizon into the first T years (say), and the period thereafter.[9] While it is not possible to quantify the social welfare loss for the above models, we have seen that whatever the length of the horizon, and 20, 25, and 30 years have been used, the optimal policy over approximately the first half of the horizon is reasonably stable and a deceleration of investment (falling scale of the 'last' plant) only takes place towards the end of the finite horizon.

One is therefore justified in concluding that the results seem operationally useful and provide valuable information of capital budget commitments for the near future. However, one must reiterate the proviso that the optimal policies are as good as the underlying data.

Furthermore, from the point of view of current planning, what matters is what should be done now and in the near future, say within a national five-year plan. Thus for Zambia, the computations here considered suggest that a steel plant should not feature within the current Second National Development Plan, 1972-76. But it probably should feature in the Third National Development Plan. Also, on the basis of current information – which may change over time – a second steel plant would be a possibility for the Fifth Plan.

8.4 Conclusions

In this chapter two models were computed on the basis of parameters estimated in Chapter 7. Model Two differed from Model One in that in the former technological change was introduced. Each model was computed for two sets of data.

Model One proved to be very sensitive to differences in the time rates of change of import price and domestic costs of production. When the import price falls at 2 per cent or 3 per cent p.a., then depending on the cost level, it is optimal to invest immediately or not at all. When the import price falls at 1/2 per cent p.a., and average unit cost of productions is $223/MT, a first plant with a capacity of 290,000 MT should come on stream in the year 8. The full demand growth range does not increase the scale of the first plant by more than 14 per cent. Due to the influence of a finite horizon, higher demand growth rates lead to a deceleration of investment towards the end of the horizon.

There is an optimal backlogging time between the first and the second plants of at least four years.

To justify immediate investment, average unit costs of production must be $212/MT or less for a plant of capacity 220,000 MT.

Alternatively, initial demand has to be some 28 per cent higher than the 1973 estimate found in Chapter 7.

When, in Model Two, technological change is introduced, the knife-edge characteristic of Model One disappears. The first plant should then come on stream between year 5 and year 8 and its scale depends on β, the demand growth rate. When $\beta = 6\%$, the scale is between 270,000 MT and 310,000 MT; when $\beta = 10\%$, the scale is between 330,000 MT and 360,000 MT. To justify immediate investment, for a plant of size 210,000 MT, average unit costs of production have to be as low as $198 per MT.

The optimal policy over approximately the first half of the horizon – or the first two plants – is reasonably stable with respect to changes in the length of the time horizon. The computed policies can therefore be treated as approximations of 'agreeable plans'.

Taking the results as a whole, two observations can be made. The first plant that is built is generally slightly larger than the demand in that year, though the plant is never more than two years ahead of demand. The second plant, too, is two to three years ahead of demand, but never more than four years ahead of demand. The results are therefore in agreement with Manne's [23] rebuttal of Chenery's [9] 'permanent excess capacity hypothesis' (see Chapter 3).

Finally, it is necessary to end on a note of caution. Dynamic Programming solutions are functions of initial parameters and small changes in them can lead to very large changes in optimal solutions. This is amply illustrated by the knife-edge characteristic of Model One. It was in the main for this very reason that a fairly wide ranging sensitivity analysis was undertaken. The initial levels of demand, import price and costs of production together with their respective rates of change turn out to be crucial for both timing and scale of plants.

In the next chapter, Model Two is extended to social cost benefit theory.

Notes

1. Dore, op. cit.
2. I am grateful to M.F.G. Scott for pointing this out to me.
3. An estimate of the general rate of inflation in Zambia was obtained by regressing in log-linear form the combined High and Low Income Price Index for 1962-71, with 1962 set to equal 100:

$$Y = 91.04e^{0.0527t}_{(0.0028)} \qquad (R^2 = 0.9763)$$

This estimated rate of inflation of 5.2% is not difference from estimates of OECD export price inflation (see Dore, *op. cit.,* for details).

4. All computations were carred out on the Oxford University computer, ICL 1906A.

5. In the model a one-year time lag is assumed between investment and capacity.

6. It is shown in Dore, *op. cit.,* that updating the average unit cost given in the ENERGOPROJEKT Report [43] for a plant size of 200,000 MT yields a figure of $239/MT. Thus it is unlikely that the figure given above is an overestimate.

7. Numerically, if an initial price of $300/MT falls at 3% p.a., then in five years it is $266, and $299 within ten years. At the end of the horizon, i.e., year 20, it falls to just $169.

8. If an initial price of $300/MT falls at 1/2% p.a., then in five years it is $294; in ten years it is $286, and in 20 years, $272.

9. 'The appropriate time-horizon is presumably always very long; but we do not care to consider exactly how long. If we would choose more or less the same policy whatever particular long time-horizon we used, there is no need for further thought on the matter: people with diverse views about the time-horizon should be able to agree, more or less, about a policy, so long as they agree that the time-horizon should be far away. More precisely, we should expect agreement about the desirability of a particular policy if, whatever the (long) time-horizon postulated, no great improvement upon that policy is possible. We call such a policy, and the growth path generated by it, *agreeable,* . . .' Mirrlees and Hammond [26], *op. cit.*

9 AN EXTENSION OF THE MODEL TO SOCIAL COST BENEFIT THEORY AND COMPUTATIONAL RESULTS

The model developed and computed in the preceding pages is concerned with dynamic optimisation of investment when there are known economies of scale both in investment and operating costs. The result is a time-phasing of capacity and imports. The basic problem was as follows: given that demand for steel grows exogenously, what course of action minimises all sacrifices?

While still remaining within the framework of partial equilibrium, a reduction in the level of abstraction is possible in at least two directions, viz. a disaggregation of the model, and/or its incorporation within the framework of modern social cost-benefit theory.[1]

A disaggregation of the model can be achieved by considering the individual components of the entire process. For the direct reduction technology under consideration this would involve six components: iron ore preparation unit, pelletisation unit, reduction unit, steel-making unit, continuous casting and finally rolling. The economies of scale parameter for each unit would have to be known: even if these parameters were known, the disaggregation would involve six state variables and six decision variables – a computationally impossible task at the present state of the art.

The second direction is to recast the model, in its present aggregated form, within the framework of social cost-benefit theory. This involves a minimum of conceptual spadework together with some rough estimate of the appropriate 'shadow' costs of production for Zambia. Section 9.1 is a very brief restatement of the principles of social valuation. In Section 9.2 Model Two of Chapter 4 is reformulated to incorporate these principles and the computed results are given.

9.1 Principles of Social Valuation

In this chapter, Model Two, developed in Chapter 4, is embraced within social cost-benefit theory. First, some principles of the theory are restated very briefly. This is followed in the next section by a revaluation of a slightly altered objective functional.

The standard criterion of revaluation in social cost-benefit theory is opportunity cost. At the conceptual level, this is non-controversial; the practical problem, however, is how to measure these opportunity costs.

The approach common to both the OECD[2] and UNIDO[3] is to posit what value would be under certain ideal conditions. In the OECD approach the ideal conditions are given when optimal trade policies are pursued by a country and when the distortions in the price structure (e.g., those introduced by state intervention, by monopoly power, etc.) are at a minimum. Under such conditions the accounting price of an importable good is the marginal social import cost and the accounting price of an exportable good is its marginal social export revenue. If the good is neither importable nor exportable, it is called a non-traded good. The accounting price of a non-traded good is given by the cost of traded goods (valued at accounting prices) directly and indirectly used up in its production.

In the UNIDO approach the ideal conditions are given by the 'free' availability of the good in question (i.e., no rationing), no monopoly or monopsony power, and that the supply of the good from the project in question is marginal, i.e., the supply will not be large enough to alter the market price. If these conditions hold then the market price would be an adequate measure of consumer willingness to pay for the good. If not, the demand curve is estimated to determine the true willingness to pay. If the good is a consumer good the approach can be applied directly; if the good is an intermediate good all consumer surpluses are summed along the production chain. If the good, intermediate or consumer, really replaces imports or displaces exports, the true impact is on foreign exchange, the value of which is again based on consumer willingness to pay for foreign exchange.

It is clear that what is required in the latter approach is atomistic competition and equilibrium in the domestic market; in the former, it is equilibrium on the world market and revaluations reflect what prices would be if those conditions held. The revaluations would then reflect social opportunity costs. In addition, if domestic production is efficient vis-à-vis the 'rest of the world' (i.e., tangency of domestic 'transformation' and foreign 'offer' curves), then the two procedures must lead to identical prices. This assumption is implicit in the UNIDO procedure of calculating a shadow price of foreign exchange.

When benefits and costs of a project are revalued in this manner, both approaches require that the difference between benefits and costs be discounted at some rate; in the UNIDO approach this is the consumption rate of interest (CRI) whereas the OECD approach is to use the so-called accounting rate of interest (ARI).

Since value of goods and services is determined by consumer willingness to pay in the UNIDO method, it follows that consumption is a convenient numeraire. Therefore, all investment is revalued in terms of the contribution it makes to consumption.

In the OECD method value is determined by prices that would prevail if the country in question followed optimal trade policies with the rest of the world,[4] i.e., the prices would be 'world prices'. Given this emphasis on international trade, accumulated foreign exchange at the disposal of government turns out to be a convenient numeraire.

Finally, both approaches value unskilled labour at a 'shadow' rate which reflects its social opportunity costs and the only difference is in the choice of the numeraire (see Dasgupta [10] or Little-Mirrlees [28], pp. 358-9). Both calculations reflect a developmental bias, namely, the assumption of the sub-optimality of savings in developing countries.

In the light of the above, it should be clear that the model of Chapter 4 can be formulated within social cost-benefit framework if

(a) some rate of discount is adopted or is taken as given;
(b) the objective functional is made parallel to the net benefit criterion;
(c) the components of the objective functional are revalued at some measure of social opportunity costs;
(d) a numeraire is chosen.

The OECD approach is adopted here for three reasons. First, the unit of account for the computations in Chapter 8 was foreign exchange of constant purchasing power. But foreign exchange held is foreign exchange invested ('not consumed'). Hence implicitly the numeraire has been 'uncommitted foreign exchange in the hands of government'.

Second, in dynamically optimising the expenditure on imports, the latter were defined as

$$[d(i) - r(i)] \, m(i).$$

That is, excess demand is imported. Since $r(i)$ is domestic output, removing the brackets implies valuing it at world prices.[5]

Third, accounting prices for traded and non-traded goods for Zambia have been computed by M. Parsonage [52].

Taking all these factors together, the objective functional is least

altered if the OECD approach is adopted. Only the ARI needs some
some attention. However, a proper consideration of the appropriate
ARI would take us far afield from the nature and purpose of this
work. It is therefore proposed that ARI is taken to be 10 per cent,
i.e. the same as the rate of discount used in Chapter 8.

9.2 Results of Model Two with Shadow Prices

The standard form of social cost benefit analysis is to maximise the
difference between benefits B and the costs C, both revalued at social
opportunity costs and discounted to the present. More formally

$$\text{Max } [B - C] = \int_0^T [Q_t - C_t - W_t - K_t] e^{-\lambda t} dt \tag{9.1}$$

where

Q_t is the output of the project (at time t)
C_t is the sum of non-wage costs
W_t is the unskilled wage bill
K_t is the capital
λ is the ARI

and where Q_t, C_t, and W_t are valued at social opportunity costs.
Since

$$\text{Max } [B - C] = \text{Min } [C - B] = J$$

the equivalent formulation of the objective functional is

$$\text{Min } J = \int_0^T [\overline{u}(i) - r(i) + br(i)m(i) + z(i)x(i) - \overline{V}_T] e^{-\lambda i} di \tag{9.2}$$

where $\overline{u}(i)$ is the capital costs of which the local cost component is
revalued at accounting prices, and

$z(i) = G \cdot c(i) \times SCF,$[6]
$\overline{V}_T$ = terminal capital stock, valued at accounting prices.

It is clear that, apart from the valuation of capital, terminal capital
and production cost at accounting prices, equation (9.2) differs from
the objective functional of Chapter 8 in that instead of *adding* imports,

+ [d(i) − r(i)] m(i)

in equation (9.2), domestic output is deducted. However, when demand d(i) is exogenously given, imports and domestic output are complements since they are both valued at the same prices: when one is determined, the other is given. Therefore equation (9.2) is conceptually identical with the objective functional of Chapter 8. Thus it does not matter whether one maximises net present value or minimises all sacrifices, as defined in Chapter 4. The only difference then is the 'shadow' valuation of capital, production costs and terminal capital.

In this chapter, Model Two is recomputed at accounting prices. The results, for the two categories of data, are given in Table 9.1. For the first category of data, viz. σ = −3%, the demand and optimal timing and scale of plants are shown in Figs. 9.1 to 9.3. The following observations may be made on these results.

First, the timing and scale of the first plant. In the previous chapter (Tables 8.8 and 8.9) the timing of the first plant is between years 5 and 8, whereas in Table 9.1, the timing is between years 3 and 5. The scale here is between 240,000 MT and 330,000 MT, compared to a range of 270,000 to 360,000 MT. In other words, the scale of the first plant is smaller than before.

Second, the period of back-logging is longer than before. In Table 9.1, the period is between four and seven years after the first plant compared to three and six years in Chapter 8.

Third, the timing and scale of the second plant. The timing is between years 9 and 14 in Table 9.1, whereas in Chapter 8, it is between years 10 and 15. While the timing range is much the same, the scale of the second plant is much larger. Whereas the scale of the second plant was between 210,000 and 370,000 MT in Chapter 8, here it is between 250,000 and 370,000 MT. The larger scale found here is due partly to a higher valuation of terminal capital.

It is reassuring to note that both the timing and scale of the first plant are unaffected by increasing the length of the time horizon to 30 years, as shown in Table 9.2. Thus the investment plan relating to the first ten years can again be treated as an 'agreeable plan', in the Mirrlees-Hammond sense.

9.3 Conclusion

It was shown here that the basic model of Chapter 4 can be

Table 9.1: Model Two, With Accounting Prices[a]

| | PLANT 1 | | | PLANT 2 | | | | PLANT 3 | | | | PLANT 4 | | | | |
| | t*₁ | Invest. $ m | Scale '000MT | No. of Years' Back-Logging t*₂ | | Invest. $ m | Scale '000MT | No. of Years' Back-Logging t*₃ | | Invest. $ m | Scale '000MT | No. of Years' Back-Logging t*₄ | | Invest. $ m | Scale '000MT | f*c US $ m |
β	t^*_1				t^*_2				t^*_3				t^*_4			
Part One, σ = −3%																
6%	5	93.4	260	7	14	69.6	250			—				—		509.51
8%	5	99.7	290	6	12	74.2	310			—				—		586.55
10%	5	107.8	330	4	11	96.4	370	0	14	60.9	200	0	18	55.7	200	603.39
Part Two, σ = −½%																
6%	3	99.4	240	7	12	97.3	250			—				—		558.73
8%	3	101.9	250	5	10	118.3	340	0	15	83.4	200			—		527.64
10%	3	106.7	270	4	9	121.4	390	0	14	84.7	200	0	17	83.6	200	659.95

a. All other parameters as given in Chapter 8, Section 8.1.
b. t* refers to optimal timing of plants.
c. f* is the optimised value of the objective functional.

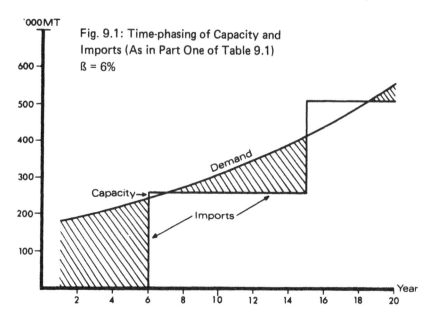

Fig. 9.1: Time-phasing of Capacity and Imports (As in Part One of Table 9.1) ß = 6%

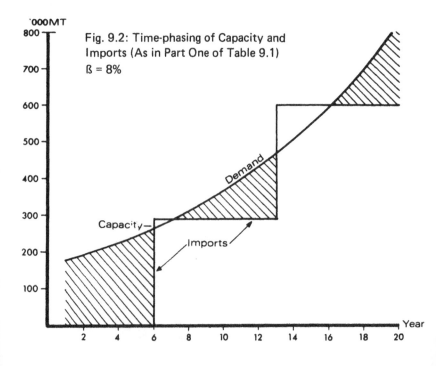

Fig. 9.2: Time-phasing of Capacity and Imports (As in Part One of Table 9.1) ß = 8%

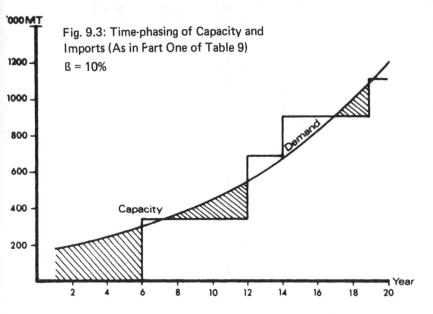

Fig. 9.3: Time-phasing of Capacity and Imports (As in Part One of Table 9)

ß = 10%

incorporated within social cost-benefit theory. This presented a choice of a numeraire and an accounting rate of interest. In order to keep the required changes to a minimum, uncommitted foreign exchange was chosen as the numeraire and production costs valued at the accounting prices for Zambia.

The use of accounting prices brings the timing of the first plant forward by about three years and the scale of the plant is of course smaller. The accounting prices are those calculated by M. Parsonage [52]. When these were calculated, the latest available Input-Output Table for Zambia was that for 1967. Since then very rapid changes have taken place in the structure of Zambia's economy and its foreign trade and so it would probably be best to regard the accounting prices as somewhat dated. However, Parsonage's paper is the only available attempt to calculate the accounting prices for Zambia.

The base year for this and the previous chapter was the year 1973. Now if it is assumed that the long-term demand growth rate is more likely to be in the 6 per cent to 8 per cent range, then the first plant should come on stream between 1976 and 1978, using the accounting prices (i.e., based on the results of this chapter). On the basis of the previous chapter, the first plant should come on stream between 1978 and 1981. In the concluding chapter, the building of the first plant is

Table 9.2: Model Two with Accounting Prices[a] — Sensitivity in the Length of the Horizon

Horizon: Years	PART 1				PART 2				PART 3				PART 4			
	t^*_1	Invest. Scale $ m	'000MT	No. of Years' Back-Logging	t^*_2	Invest. Scale $ m	'000MT	No. of Years' Back-Logging	t^*_3	Invest. Scale $ m	'000MT	No. of Years' Back-Logging	t^*_4	Invest. Scale $ m	'000MT	f^* '000MT US $ m
Part One, $\sigma = -3\%$:																
20	5	93.4	260	7	14	69.6	250	2	23	—	270					509.51
30	5	93.4	260	7	14	88.1	370	2	23	55.7	270					613.10
Part Two, $\sigma = -\frac{1}{2}\%$																
20	3	99.4	240	7	12	97.4	250	0	21	—	210					558.73
30	3	99.4	240	8	13	122.6	370	0	21	83.9	210	3	29	78.2	200	326.24

a. All other parameters as given in Chapter 8, Section 8.1.

considered more concretely and several realistic aspects are introduced. It is hoped that this will show how the more abstract analysis of the previous pages is usable for practical work.

Notes

1. This is not the place to justify the contention that the vast and growing literature on social cost-benefit analysis and project evaluation can be neatly unified and presented as a single theory. Yet from the earliest work of Dupuit and Hotelling, through the work of the US Government on the public benefit of water-resources development in the 1930s, to the modern formulations of social cost-benefit analysis in the publications of the OECD and UNIDO, there is one common search, namely the search for (social) value, which may or may not be wholly reflected in price. And with the latter publications it has become clear that there is yet another dimension to social value, and that is value judgment(s). Social cost-benefit theory has become less and less cut and dried than it was once thought. The teleological implications of the theory are now explicitly stated, making economic rationality more of a tool and less of a master.
2. OECD Manual by Little and Mirrlees [28].
3. UNIDO Guidelines by Dasgupta, Marglin and Sen [35].
4. Of course, ultimately, these prices represent international willingness to pay.
5. The determination of domestic willingness to pay for steel proved to be rather difficult because in Zambia (a) over the past three years steel has been subsidized by the state and consequently (b) it has been rationed, and (c) the two mining giants have monopsony power. In short, all the required UNIDO assumptions were violated.
6. SCF stands for the Standard Conversion Factor (Little and Mirrlees [28]).

10 THE PLANNING PROBLEM IN PERSPECTIVE

The computational results of the last two chapters do not of course complete the 'applied' aspect of the dynamic investment planning problem. It is only by taking a much closer look at the case study can one hope to reduce the level of abstraction so that the theoretical model comes to life with immediate empirical relevance for the decision-maker. Thus 'dynamics' must be shown to blend well with practice before the decision-maker can be persuaded to take the analysis seriously.

Consequently, the purpose of this chapter is to introduce certain doses of realism into the planning problem by taking a disaggregated look at a steel complex, in the light of the main conclusions of the last two chapters. But before doing this, it might be worth restating two principal findings of this work at a 'higher' level of abstraction. First, it was found that small scale alternatives to the BF-BOS technique exist for developing countries and, second, on the basis of computations presented here, it seems advisable to earmark funds for a steel plant with a scale of 290,000-300,000 MT for Zambia for the Third National Development Plan, 1977-81, to come on stream towards the end of the TNDP, i.e., 1980-81. In what follows, this will simply be referred to as the *first plant*.

An integrated steel plant based on DR-EF has six main production units: (1) mining, (2) pelletising unit, (3) direct reduction unit, (4) electric-arc furnace, (5) continuous casting machine, and (6) rolling mill. On the one hand, this description suggests a degree of flexibility in the build-up of such a plant but, on the other hand, it is obvious that there must be some physical 'balance' in the capacities of the production units: each successive unit must not have a capacity smaller than the 'output' of the previous unit in the chain.

However, due to economies of scale and due to the fact that investment in each unit is lumpy, the entire production process is normally characterised by a considerable degree of 'overdimensioning'. Entrepreneurs anticipate future increases in demand too, and therefore provide for a possible expansion of the plant by overdimensioning. This leads to the erosion of a part of the expected economies of scale in operating costs. But this is not all; unfortunately for developing countries, this overdimensioning persists even when the plant has had to be expanded in successive stages. Tables 10.1 is a typical small semi-integrated plant based on scrap that a developing country might consider. The table is based on the assumption that demand would double every eight years and that a three-stage expansion of the single plant is spread over 12 years. From the percentage utilisation column of Table 10.1, it is clear that the maximum benefits in the economies of scale in the operating costs cannot be achieved for a very long time.

The Zambian first plant need not necessarily be a fully integrated steel plant. Indeed, in practice there are at least four variants that may be considered by the decision-maker. These are now discussed below briefly to put the practical planning problem into perspective.

10.1 Variant I

The first possibility is to consider a rolling mill only. Some developing countries have followed this course, for example, Kenya and Uganda. In theory, it is also possible to install a rolling mill with a view to 'backward integration' later. However, such a development plan will almost certainly involve overdimensioning, in which case it might be optimal to simply delay the entire plan, i.e., postpone investment until such time as when an integrated plant becomes viable.

Rolling mills vary from simple units to fully automatic installations as annual capacity increases from 25,000 MT to 300,000 MT. Table 10.2 gives the investment and production costs per MT for three plant sizes. Taking the 200,000 MT unit plant as a basis for comparison, one can see that for a mill of size 100,000 MT, investment and production costs would be some 20 per cent higher; whereas for a mill with an annual capacity of 300,000 MT, unit investment cost is reduced by 14 per cent and unit production costs by 11 per cent.

As a matter of fact a feasibility study[1] for a rolling mill for Zambia was carried out by a Japanese consortium in 1973. This study — to be

Table 10,2: Rolling Mill Only[a]

Annual Capacity in MT	Investment Cost /MT	Production Cost /MT
100,000	$ 316	$ 125
200,000	264	105
300,000	227	93.5

Source: UNIDO [79]

a. The cost estimates are based on 1967 data.

Table 10.1: Successive Stages of Expansion and Percentage Utilization of Semi-Integrated Steel Plant Producing Non-Flat Products[a]

Equipment	Annual Capacity in MT	Annual Production in MT	Percentage Utilisation of Capacity	No. of 8 hr. Shifts/Week
First Stage:				
1 electric arc furnace, 34 MT capacity	110,000	85,000	78	15
1 continuous casting machine with 3 strands	245,000	81,000	33	15
1 semi-continuous rolling mill for bars and light sections	290,000	72,000	25	5
Second Stage: (4 years later)				
2 electric arc furnaces, each 34 MT capacity	220,000	170,000	78	15
1 continuous casting machine with 3 strands	245,000	162,000	66	15
1 semi-continuous rolling mill for bars and light sections	290,000	144,000	50	10
Third Stage: (4 years later)				
3 electric arc furnaces, each of 34 MT capacity	330,000	255,000	78	15
1 continuous casting machine with 3 strands	490,000	243,000	50	15
1 semi-continuous rolling mill for bars and light sections	290,000	216,000	75	15

Source: UNIDO [78], p.22.

a. Assuming demand doubles every eight years.

called the Itoh Report in this book — recommended the establishment of a mill with an annual capacity of 25,000 MT. It would rely on imported Japanese billets and roll only three basic primary steel products, viz. merchant bars, deformed bars and equal angles.

The investment cost per MT was $328 which is rather high, but of the total investment of US $8.2m, Zambian equity capital was to be only $2.5m — the balance was to be provided by the consortium in the form of a deferred loan.[2]

If the objective is eventually to build up an integrated plant that would use local resources, in a planned way, then the small mill is unlikely to be suitable for future integration. If a small mill is accepted, an integrated steel plant would have to be postponed for a very long time or until export possibilities become feasible.

Furthermore, as shown in Chapter 7, the economies of scale in the rolling of shaped steel products are concentrated within the range of 100,000 MT to 500,000 MT. There seems very little case for recommending Variant I for Zambia. Even if all other variants are rejected, it seems that a much larger mill must be contemplated, with a possible five-year delay, so that the mill is in the 300,000 MT to 500,000 MTPY range.

10.2 Variant II

A second possibility for Zambia is to consider a semi-integrated steel plant — what is currently called a 'mini-steel plant'. This would have three production units: a scrap using electric arc furnace, a continuous casting machine and a semi-continuous rolling mill.

Even developed countries are establishing mini-steel plants, especially the smaller firms, as they compete with the very large scale, computerised production plants of large firms. India, too, has recently established seven such mini-steel plants.

The crucial factor for such plants is the ready availability of steel scrap. International trade in scrap is highly volatile and the price of scrap fluctuates so wildly — except when domestically controlled[3] — that it cannot realistically be a basis for a new plant in Zambia. The supply of domestic scrap[4] in Zambia is rather low but, in any case, it is entirely earmarked for the steel foundry manufacturing grinding media for the copper mines.

However, to complete the investment cost picture Table 10.3 below and Table 7.4 (p.84) may be consulted (it will be recalled that the latter table refers to plants in the UK only). Table 10.3 gives the investment costs of three Indian plants studied in 1973. The same study also estimated that the production cost per MT of billets in a 100,000 MT plant was $105.

Table 10.3: Capital Cost[a] of Electric Arc Furnace(s) and Continuous Casting Machine(s)

Billet Production MTPY	No. and Capacity of Electric arc Furnaces	No. of Continuous Casting Machines and Its Strands	Total Estimated Investment Cost per MT
50,000	2 x 10-12 MT	1 (2 strands)	$ 93.4
100,000	2 x 20-25 MT	1 (4 strands)	80.0
150,000	3 x 20-25 MT	2 (4 strands)	88.9[b]

Source: Banerjee and Silgardo [60].

a. The capital cost does not include the capital cost of auxiliary service departments.
b. The unit investment cost is higher because of considerable excess capacity on the second continuous casting machine.

This particular variant would only be relevant for Zambia if:
(a) Variant I was accepted initially, and (b) it was decided later to 'import substitute' the billets used by the rolling mill. In this case it must be assumed that the problem of the feed for the arc furnaces (steel scrap or pig iron or sponge iron) has been satisfactorily solved.

10.3 Variant III

The third possibility is to export prereduced ore (i.e., 30%-70% Fe), or pelletised ore, until it is optimal to 'integrate forward', by adding on electric arc furnace(s), continuous casting machine(s) and a rolling mill. The export of prereduced ore or pellets would have to compete with other major exporters who have access to the sea, e.g. Angola, Liberia, Venezuela, Canada, and Australia. Given Zambia's land-locked position, this possibility is largely hypothetical.

10.4 Variant IV

The fourth possibility is an integrated steel plant based on the DR-EF route. This is the only possibility that will not only utilise the large and high quality Zambian iron ore deposits, but will secure the maximum advantages of the economies of scale in iron-making, steel-making, continuous casting and rolling of primary steel products.

On the basis of parameters estimated in Chapter 7, the dynamic investment planning models computed in Chapters 8 and 9 suggest that a first plant should come on stream around 1980/81, with a scale of about 290,000 MT to 310,000 MT.

As mentioned before, the Zambian Government has decided to establish a DR-EF steel plant.[5] The plant would take three years to build,[6] and commercial quality production would begin in 1977. Total production is expected to be 90,000 MT in 1977, 170,000 MT in 1978, and the capacity production of 200,000 MT in 1979.

Table 10.4 gives the description of the steel products, the quantity to be produced after 1979, and the price for each product. Also given is the CIF landed cost for each of these products (in October 1973). The table shows that the prices at which the feasibility study values the output of the proposed plant are, on the whole, considerably below the average import price. This anomaly has risen as follows. ENERGOPROJEKT asked a civil servant in Mindeco (a state enterprise) to produce a schedule of prices at which the products of the proposed plant would sell. The civil servant produced the current price list, controlled (and frozen since 1971) by the government. It is obvious that these government controlled prices are totally unrealistic, since in November 1973, Steel Supplies of Zambia (also a state enterprise) urged the Ministry of Trade and Industry to allow a price increase, as their import costs exceeded the government controlled steel prices. Steel Supplies, of course, pointed out that they were making losses as a result of the controlled prices.

Table 10.4: Commodity Composition. Target Quantities and Prices for the Output of Proposed Steel Plant

Description	Quantity MT	Price $/MT	CIF Import Cost/MT
Wire Rod	10,000	$ 295	$ 391-241
Reinforcing bar	90,000	295	395-240
Rods and Bars	55,000	310	409
Light shapes	45,000	335	353-425
	200,000		
Average revenue per MT of output: $ 308.12			
Average CIF import price[a] per MT: $ 386.00			

Sources: ENERGOPROJEKT Report [43] and Steel Supplies of Zambia Ltd., memorandum dated 9th November 1973

a. This average takes the commodity composition of demand into account.

Table 10.5 gives the basic information on annual capacity of each production unit and the percentage of capacity utilisation. In this connection, it should be noted that in practice, about 90 per cent of capacity utilisation is satisfactory, due to work stoppages for a variety of reasons. This means that only the continuous casting machine and the rolling mill are overdimensioned and will have spare capacity.

The capacity of the Hyl direct reduction unit can be increased by 25 per cent by adding on a fifth vessel. This will be necessary quite soon after the plant has started producing 200,000 MT. The increase in the capacity of the reduction unit will bring the rolling mill to near full capacity operation, although there will still be spare capacity in the four strand continuous casting machine.

The 25 per cent increase in the capacity of the reduction unit might also require an additional electric arc furnace — which could be made in Zambia,[7] when necessary. Indeed, with the chronic shortage of steel scrap in Zambia, a larger reduction unit might even supplement — with sponge iron — the raw material requirement of the seven foundries of Zambia.

The investment costs corresponding to the equipment in Table 10.5 is given in Table 10.6, together with the proportionate share of each unit in the total equipment cost. Two observations may be made here.

First, note that before continuous casting was invented, a blooming mill absorbed about 20 per cent of the total cost of installed equipment. This invention, like the discovery of direct reduction, has helped to put the smaller integrated plant within reach of the resources and demand levels of developing countries.

Second, note that in Table 10.6, the pelletising plant absorbs a quarter of total equipment cost. Unfortunately, the ENERGOPROJEKT Report does not make an absolutely convincing case for the need for pelletisation of Zambian ore. Swindell-Dressler Company, the owners of the patent rights for the Hyl direct reduction process and also the consultant engineers for the Zambian project, have carried out reducibility tests on Zambian iron ore.[8] This report shows that lumps of Zambian iron ore may be used as feed for the Hyl plant but would result in losses of iron as the lump has a tendency to disintegrate.

J.R. Miller [69] gives data that shows that the unit comprehensive production costs per MT of raw steel is lower for gaseous direct reduction with pellet than with lump. However, the cost difference is very small for the plant size under consideration. The cost difference is a full $1.00 per MT only for a plant of 500,000 MT. Only for much

Table 10.5: Proposed Integrated Steel Plant (DR-EF)

	Annual Capacity in MT	Annual Production in MT	Percentage of Capacity Utilisation	No. of 8-hour Working Shifts per week
Equipment				
Mining[a]	a	350,000	–	10
Crushing, grinding and pelletising	365,000	332,000	91	21
1 Reduction unit (Hyl)[b]	240,000	215,000	90	21
2 50-MT electric arc furnaces[c]	300,000	270,000	90	20
1 Continuous casting machine with 4 strands	470,000	218,000	46[d]	10
1 Semi-continuous rolling mill for bars, rods and light sections	307,700	200,000	65	16

Source: ENERGOPROJEKT Report [43].

a. Mining is of the 'open-pit' type, and so annual capacity is variable, being a function of men and their machines.

b. The Hyl direct reduction unit is made up of four reaction vessels. It is possible to add a fifth vessel and raise its annual capacity by 25%.

c. The capacity as well as output of the EF furnaces is greater than its input from the 'previous' unit in the chain because of recycled steel scrap from within the integrated steel plant. Assumed average 'heat time' 3 hrs.; produces 50 MT of molten steel every 3 hours.

d. Assuming an average casting speed of 60 MT per hour.

Table 10.6: Investment by Production Units for the Proposed Steel Plant

Equipment	Investment '000 US $	Percentage of Total Investment
Mining	$ 1,455	3%
Pelletising plant	18,416	25
Reduction plant	18,072	25
Steel shop	7,165	10
Continuous casting	5,312	7
Bar and Rod Mill	21,235	30
TOTAL EQUIPMENT:	$71,655	100%
Royalties	$ 675	
Site facilities and average spares inventory	5,145	
Pre-operating costs (training and administration)	2,215	
Working capital (including inventories)	3,026	
	$ 82,716	
10% addition[a] for possible errors and omissions	8,271	
	$ 90,987	

Source: ENERGOPROJEKT Report [43].

a. Not included in the Report.

larger plant sizes is the cost reduction due to pelletisation significant.

The Swindell-Dressler report finds that pelletised Zambian iron ore would make an 'excellent' feed for an Hyl plant and that it would increase the production rate and also decrease unit gas consumption. It concludes: 'the cost of pelletisation is more than compensated by the saving realised in the reduction plant performance'. But no evidence is given to support this conclusion.

From Table 10.7 it can be seen that pelletisation adds $12.39 per

MT to production cost. Therefore, without pelletisation, unit reduction costs must exceed $76, i.e., taking pelletisation and reduction cost together. But even simple arithmetic of this kind is missing from the ENERGOPROJEKT Report so that it is not possible to economically evaluate the pelletisation. Ideally, one would want a complete cash flow both with and without the pelletisation unit to judge the merits of the two cases.

Furthermore, it will be remembered (from Table 10.5) that there will be considerable excess capacity in the continuous casting machine and the rolling mill. If the whole integrated plant is delayed as recommended here, further reductions in the unit cost of production may be expected. Even assuming that the unit cost reduction on casting is ignored, if the rolling mill is operated at 90 per cent of capacity, a saving in average cost of rolling of just over $5 per MT can be expected.

Lastly, it is clear from Table 10.7 that the price of naphtha is of crucial importance. In 1972 the f.o.b. price of naphtha was $3.40 per barrel. In February, 1975, it had risen to $12.60 per barrel (f.o.b.). The gas is pumped through the TAZAMA pipeline which runs from the oil refinery at Ndola (in Zambia) to the port of Dar es Salaam in Tanzania. When an appropriate portion of freight cost ($3.40/MT) and the pipeline tariff (K 16.00 per MT) is added, the CIF cost per barrel of naphtha comes to $16.35. This is equivalent to $3.44 per MM BTU.[9] (However, there is a debate going on in Zambia on whether to gasify Zambian coal or whether naphtha should be manufactured at the oil refinery from the heavy oil residue, which has to be used up somehow, if the oil refinery is to continue operating.)

Now assuming that the current (i.e., February 1975) price of naphtha might rise by a further 35 per cent, then this doubles the *original* price of $2.33/MM BTU used in the ENERGOPROJEKT Report – see Table 10.7. Such a further rise in price will add $49.07 per MT to the average cost of production and bring it to $203.89. (This price is about 2.7 times the cost given by Miller.)

Finally, the profitability analysis of the proposed project will be discussed. Table 10.8 gives the cash flow for the first three years after start up, i.e., after the three-year construction period. Year 3 after start up is representative of the cash flow for the remaining 12 years of the life of the plant. The cash flow assumes that the percentage of capacity utilisation will be the same – apart from the first two years after start up – as that given in Table 10.5. No expansion of any of the production units has been allowed for in this cash flow. This is of

Table 10.7: Unit Investment and Production Costs for the Proposed Steel Plant in Zambia

Production Unit	Investment per MT	Operating Cost per MT	Fixed Cost per MT	Average Cost of Production per MT
Mining	$ 4.15	$ 2.17	$ 0.30	$ 2.47
Pelletisation	50.45	8.43	3.96	12.39
Reduction	97.53	53.33[b] (102.37)[c]	11.05[d]	64.38
Melt shop	31.20[a]	29.53	4.22	33.75
Continuous casting	–	9.12	3.47	12.59
Rolling mill	69.16	21.64	7.60	29.24
TOTAL PER MIT:		$ 124.22	$ 25.60	$ 154.82

Source: ENERGOPROJEKT Report [43].

a. Includes cost of continuous casting machine.
b. Assumes naphtha price of $2.33/MM BTU as in the original report.
c. Assuming the price of naphtha doubles, i.e., $4.66/MM BTU. (Current CIF price of naphtha is $3.44/MM BTU.)
d. Includes royalty on Hyl plant.

Table 10.8: Revenue and Expenditure for the Proposed Steel Plant ('000 US $)

	Years after Start Up		
	1	2	3
Production, MTPY			
1. Wire rod	5,000	8,500	10,000
2. Reinforcing bar	45,000	76,500	90,000
3. Rods and bars	27,500	46,800	55,000
4. Light shapes	22,500	38,300	45,000
REVENUE:			
1. Wire bar $295/MT	1,475	2,508	2,950
2. Reinforcing bar $295/MT	13,275	22,568	26,550
3. Rods and bars $310/MT	8,525	14,508	17,050
4. Light shapes	7,538	12,831	15,075
TOTAL REVENUE:	30,813	52,415	61,625
PRODUCTION COSTS:			
1. Operating costs — mining, pelletising, reducing:			
(a) Labour and Supervision	1,254	1,254	1,254
(b) Raw materials and supplies	9,993	12,491	12,491
2. Operating costs — steel-making, casting, rolling:			
(a) Labour and Supervision	1,809	1,809	1,809
(b) Raw materials and supplies (with scrap credit)	5,573	8,360	9,289
3. Commissioning expenses	759	200	—
4. Depreciation	5,120	5,120	5,120
5. Interest	7,882	7,094	6,306
	32,381	36,128	36,269
NET CASH FLOW:	− 1,568	+ 16,287	+ 25,356

Source: ENERGOPROJEKT Report [43].

course a serious limitation of the feasibility study prepared by ENERGOPROJEKT.

Assuming that the $90m capital expenditure is spread equally over the three-year construction period, then the cash flow in Table 10.8 gives an internal rate of return of 15 per cent. The rate of discount used in the public sector project analysis in Zambia is 10 per cent.

It will be noted from Tables 10.8 and 10.4 given above (pp. 149 and 143) that the output prices are on the whole below the corresponding CIF import costs: average revenue has been understated by some 25 per cent. On the other hand, the price of naphtha has risen by about 47 per cent since the study was made.

Assume now that:

(1) total revenue can be increased by 25 per cent,
(2) the price of naphtha increases to $4.66/MM BTU
   (i.e., twice the level assumed in the ENERGOPROJEKT Report), and
(3) other petroleum based inputs (lubricants, furnace oil, petrol, etc.) also double in price from the levels assumed in the ENERGOPROJEKT Report,

it is then possible to estimate the adjusted cash flow as given in Table 10.9.

Again, if the capital expenditure is spread equally over the three-year construction period, the adjusted cash flow of Table 10.9 gives an internal rate of return of 18 per cent. Once again it is assumed that the net cash flow in year 6 is representative of the remaining 12 years of the life of the plant. Of course there are several simplifying assumptions underlying this analysis, both on the revenue and on the cost side. It could be improved if the possible expansion of the plant – as outlined above – was also taken into account. It can certainly be improved if a coherent energy policy were formulated. A by-product of such an energy policy would be a firm decision on the future of the oil refinery and on whether local coal is to be gasified for the steel plant. The above analysis is also based on the assumption that, whatever the decision, the reductant to be used in the steel plant would not cost more than the (increased) c.i.f. price of naphtha used in the above calculations.

10.5 Conclusion

The following three conclusions can be made about a steel plant for Zambia:

Table 10.9: Adjusted Cash Flow for the Proposed Steel Plant in US $ Million

	Year 1	Year 2	Year 3	Year 4	Year 5	Year 6[d]
Capital Expenditure[a]	−30.0	−30.0	−30.0			
Net profit as in Table 10.8				−1.568	+16.287	+25.356
Increase in Revenue[b]				+7.703	+13.104	+15.406
Increase in cost of Production[c]				−8.250	−10.843	−11.478
Net change				−0.547	+ 2.261	+ 3.928
NET CASH FLOW:	−30.0	−30.0	−30.0	−2.115	+18.548	+29.284

a. See Table 10.6.
b. A 25% increase in total revenue of Table 10.8.
c. Increased cost of raw materials — naphtha price and price of petroleum based inputs double the level assumed in Table 10.8.
d. Year 6 is assumed to be representative of the remaining 12 years of the life of the plant.

(1) Of the four variants briefly considered, only Variant IV, i.e., a fully integrated, DR-EF steel plant seems sensible for consideration for Zambia.

(2) The optimal scale for the first fully integrated plant is about 290,000 MT to 300,000 MT to be operated at near full capacity by 1981.

(3) The proposed steel plant for Zambia has the continuous casting unit as well as the rolling mill considerably over-dimensioned so that its rated capacity approaches the optimal scale mentioned above (see Table 10.5). However, an expansion of the reduction unit as well as an additional electric arc furnace – locally built – would seem essential in the near future to exploit the spare capacity in casting and rolling. These items should be incorporated into the cash flow.

The above conclusions are still subject to two loose ends: a decision on the reductant to be used in the steel plant (as a consequence of a rational energy policy), and an economic consideration of whether pelletisation is necessary at all.

In this chapter an attempt was made to show how fairly abstract dynamic analysis can be effectively integrated with practical decision-making concerns. The case study was pursued as far as was possible, although rather briefly. Thus not only the question of optimal timing and scale, but also the actual build-up of the plant in a number of ways were discussed. Needless to add, this is still incomplete; for instance, nothing was said about location, commodity composition of production, etc. But one hopes the general direction was exemplified.

Notes

1. *Preliminary Study for Steel Rolling Mill in the Republic of Zambia,* prepared by C. Itoh and Co. Ltd, Yodogawa Steelworks Ltd, and Rinko Seitetsu Co. Ltd, Aug. 1973 [46].
2. The Itoh Report, assuming a 12-year life of the mill and five-year tax holiday, produces a cash flow that shows a rate of return of 63% on the equity investment. (The report rejects the concept of the rate of return on total outlay.)
3. See Cockerill and Silberston [64], pp. 22-4.
4. About 40,000 MTPY are generated by the copper mines.
5. Apparently the contract has been signed and a 10% down payment was made in 1975.
6. According to UNIDO [79], the normal period of construction for an integrated steel plant in a developing country is between five and seven years.
7. The metal using sector in Zambia is fairly sophisticated, if only the government would encourage this expatriate-owned and expatriate-dominated sector.

I have, in fact, seen that the foundry in Lusaka manufactures steel parts and components in emergencies for complex machines used, e.g. by the cement factory. The foundry has also built for itself a medium-sized blast furnace. The foundry was keen to mine surface iron ore deposits for the manufacture of buildersware products – in part imported from China and Japan – but was stopped by the government. An engineering concern on the Copperbelt has built itself a simple rolling mill machine for the cold rolling of equal angles from scrapped railway track. The owner of this concern, an experienced engineer, assured me that his firm could, in cooperation with the local foundry, manufacture *de novo* an electric arc furnace of required specifications. However, government is hostile to expatriate enterprise, irrespective of its contribution to the economy. Much of the post-independence decline in the metal using sector (see Dore [13] for a detailed analysis) can be attributed to such political factors.

8. Swindell-Dressler Co., *Reducibility Evaluation of Zambian Iron Ore for Energoprojekt, Yugoslavia,* Pittsburgh, U.S.A. (undated). Appears as Annex in the ENERGOPROJEKT Report [43].

9. I am grateful to Dr Jacob Mwanza, Managing Director of the Zambia Energy Commission, for supplying this information.

11 SUMMARY AND CONCLUSION

This book is based on the assumption that for many projects the benefits that can be derived from the investment are sensitive to the time segment over which the benefits are spread out. Since the relevant time segment is always a particular time period, an explicitly dynamic optimisation framework is necessary. Such a framework is provided by dynamic programming which was in fact developed (by Bellman) with the feasibility of computation in mind.

The basic ideas of dynamic programming were illustrated in Chapter 2 with the aid of examples. It was shown that backward sequencing in DP captures the irreversibility of time. In Chapter 3 two important approaches to dynamic investment planning were surveyed and their common features were highlighted. This in turn showed up some restrictive assumptions which made the two approaches mathematically tractable.

In Chapter 4 a new model was presented. It was claimed that the new model was designed to capture some important features of reality. More specifically, these features were: (a) economies of scale in both investment and production costs; (b) a changing real price of the commodity to be produced; and (c) lumpiness of investment, i.e., discrete plant sizes, with a fairly large investment required for the minimum plant size, with subsequently larger plant sizes reflecting both technical and physical constraints. It was shown that not all technically balanced and feasible plant sizes are of economic interest.

Chapter 5 was a brief explanation of the computational algorithm. That concluded the theoretical part of the book.

Part Two of the book was oriented towards a thorough and fairly detailed application of the theory to a case study. Thus, Part Two began with a chapter on the basic information required for planning a steel industry, the chosen case study. In Chapter 7, the parameters required for computation were presented. A case was made for 'well established' parameters, because of the fact that optimal policies are a function of the initial parameters. It was for this reason too that a fairly wide ranging sensitivity analysis was reported in Chapter 8, which contains the main numerical results.

The model was then extended, in Chapter 9, to incorporate social cost benefit theory and some further numerical results were given.

Finally, in Chapter 10, it was shown that the abstract analysis of the previous chapters meshes well with the problem of investment planning in practice.

BIBLIOGRAPHY

1. Aris, R., *Discrete Dynamic Programming* (Balisdell, Waltham, Mass., 1964)
2. Arrow, K.J. and M. Kurz, *Public Investment, the Rate of Return and Optimal Fiscal Policy* (Johns Hopkins Press, Baltimore, 1970)
3. Beckman, M.J., *Dynamic Programming of Economic Decisions* (Springerverlag, Berlin, 1968)
4. Bellman, R.E and S.E. Dreyfus, *Applied Dynamic Programming* (Princeton University Press, Princeton, 1962)
5. Bostock, M. and C. Harvey (eds.), *Economic Independence and Zambian Copper: A Case Study of Foreign Investment* (Praeger, New York, 1972)
6. Chakravarty, S, *The Logic of Investment Planning* (North-Holland Publishing Co, Amsterdam, 1968)
7. Chakravarty, S., 'The Optimal Growth Path for Finite Planning Horizons', in T. Majumdar (ed.), *Growth and Choice* (Oxford University Press, London, 1969)
8. Chakravarty, S., *Capital and Development Planning* (M.I.T. Press, Cambridge, Mass., 1969)
9. Chenery, H.B., 'Overcapacity and the Acceleration Principle', *Econometrica,* January 1952.
10. Dasgupta, P., 'A Comparative Analysis of the UNIDO Guidelines and the OECD Manual', *Bulletin of the Oxford University Institute of Economics and Statistics,* Vol. 34, No. 1 (February 1972)
11. Dixit, A., J.A. Mirrlees, and N.H. Stern, 'Optimum saving with economies of scale', Oxford (mimeo), February 1974.
12. Donardo, E.V., *Dynamic Programming: Theory and Application* (McGraw Hill, New York, forthcoming 1977)
13. Dore, M.H.I., 'Planning an Iron and Steel Industry for Zambia'. Unpublished doctoral dissertation, University of Oxford, 1975.
14. Erlenkotter, D., 'Optimal Plant Size with Time-Phased Imports' in Alan Manne (ed.), *Investment for Capacity Expansion* (George Allen and Unwin, London, 1967)
15. Faber, M.L.O. and J.G. Potter (eds.), *Towards Economic Independence* (Cambridge University Press, Cambridge, 1971)

16. Fortman, B. de G., *After Mulungushi: the Economics of Zambian Humanism* (East Africa Publishing House, Nairobi, 1969)
17. Haldi, J. and D. Whitcomb, 'Economies of Scale in Industrial Plants', *Journal of Political Economy*, Vol. 75 (1967)
18. Intriligator, M.D., *Mathematical Optimization and Economic Theory* (Prentice-Hall, Englewood Cliffs, N.J., 1971)
19. Jacobs, O.L.R., *An Introduction to Dynamic Programming* (Chapman and Hall, London, 1967)
20. Jaskold-Gabszewicz, J. and J.-P. Vial, 'Optimal Capacity Expansion under Growing Demand and Technological Progress', in K. Shell and S. Szego (eds.), *Mathematical Methods in Investment and Finance* (North-Holland, Amsterdam, 1972)
21. Jaskold-Gabszewicz, J., Vial, J.-P. and C. d'Aspremont, 'Capital depreciation, growing demand and economies of scale', *CORE* DP No. 6918.
22. Little, I.M.D. and J.A. Mirrlees, *Project Appraisal and Planning for Developing Countries* (Heinemann, London, 1974)
23. Manne, A., 'Capacity Expansion and Probabilistic Growth', *Econometrica*, October 1961.
24. Manne, A., *Investments for Capacity Expansion: size, location and time-phasing* (George Allen and Unwin, London, 1967)
25. Marglin, S., *Approaches to Dynamic Investment Planning* (North-Holland Publishing Co, Amsterdam, 1963)
26. Mirrlees, J.A. and P.J. Hammond, 'Agreeable Plans', a paper for the I.E.A. Conference on Growth Models, 30 March-3 April 1970, Nuffield College.
27. Moore, F.T., 'Economies of Scale: Some Statistical Evidence', *Quarterly Journal of Economics*, Vol. 73 (1959)
28. OECD Manual: I.M.D. Little and J.A. Mirrlees, *Manual of Industrial Project Analysis in Developing Countries*, Vol. II, *Social Cost-Benefit Analysis* (Development Centre of the OECD, Paris, 1968)
29. Pontryagin, L.S., V.G. Boltyanskii, R.V. Gamkrelidze and E.F. Mishchenko, *The Mathematical Theory of Optimal Processes* (Pergamon, Oxford, 1964)
30. Sen, A.K., 'Terminal Capital and Optimum Savings' in C.H. Feinstein (ed.), *Socialism, Capitalism and Economic Growth* (Cambridge University Press, Cambridge, 1967)
31. Sengupta, J.K. and A. Sen., 'The Optimal Capacity Expansion Policy for a Multi-product Firm under a Dynamic Framework', *Metroeconomica*, Vol. 25 (April 1973)

32.   Shell-BP, Crude Oil and Natural Gas Developments in Nigeria, (Shell-BP, September 1972, mimeo)

33.   Srinivasan, T.N., 'Geometric Rate of Growth of Demand' in Alan Manne (ed.), *Investments in Capacity Expansion* (George Allen and Unwin, London, 1967)

34.   UN/ECA, *The Development of the Iron and Steel Industry in Africa* (Addis Ababa, 1963, mimeo)

35.   UNIDO Guidelines: P. Dasgupta, S. Marglin and A.K. Sen, *Guidelines for Project Evaluation* (UNIDO, United Nations, New York, 1972)

36.   Weitzman, M.L., 'Optimum growth with scale economies in the creation of overhead capital', *Review of Economic Studies,* XXXVII (4) (1970)

37.   Westphal, L.E., *Planning Investments with Economies of Scale* (North-Holland Publishing Co, Amsterdam, 1971)

Sources of Data

Zambian Sources

38.   Annual Census of Production. (Central Statistical Office, Lusaka, 1965 to 1971)

39.   Annual Statement of External Trade. (Central Statistical Office, Lusaka, 1945-53 and 1964-72)

40.   Bank of Zambia. Report and Statement of Accounts for the year ended 31 December 1973.

41.   Bechtel. Zambian Steel Project Development Report. (Bechtel International Corporation, San Francisco, April 1971)

42.   Building Industry and the National Development Plan, The. (Office of National Development and Planning, Lusaka, 1967)

43.   ENERGOPROJEKT. Feasibility Study for Integrated Steelworks in Zambia. (Energoprojekt, Beograd, Yugoslavia, August 1973)

44.   Garlick, W., Lusaka Iron Ore Deposits (unpublished file at the Department of Geological Survey), Lusaka, 1949.

45.   INDECO-MINDECO. Steel Marketing Survey, Indeco and Mindeco, March 1974 (mimeo).

46.   ITOH. Preliminary Study for Steel Rolling Mill in the Republic of Zambia, prepared by C. Itoh and Co. Ltd, Yodogawa Steelworks Ltd and Rinko Seitetsu Co. Ltd, August 1973, referred in the book as the Itoh Report.

47.   Jolly, R. and M. Williams, 'Macro-Budget Policy in an Open Export Economy: Lessons from Zambian Experience', *Eastern Africa Economic Review,* Vol. 4, No. 2 (December 1972)

48. Kaunda, Kenneth, 'Take up the Challenge', (Zambia Information Services, Lusaka, 1970)
49. Maxwell Stamp Associates. Pre-investment Study of the Copper Fabricating Industry in the East and Central African Sub-region. (Maxwell Stamp, London 1969, mimeo)
50. Monthly Digest of Statistics (of Zambia), Central Statistical Office, Vol. X, No. 7, July 1974.
51. National Accounts and Input-Output Tables of Zambia, 1965-67 and 1969 (Central Statistical Office, Lusaka)
52. Parsonage, M.A., 'Employment, Wages and Shadow Prices in Zambia' (Nuffield College, Oxford, 1973, mimeo)
53. Second National Development Plan (Ministry of Development Planning and National Guidance, Zambia, 1971)
54. Société d'études et de réalisations industrielles Renault engineering. Situation and Development Prospects of the Metal-Working Industries in Zambia, Vols. I-III, February 1969 (mimeo), referred to throughout the text as SERIECO Report.
55. Some Important Tables of Urban Budget Survey, 1966-68. (Central Statistical Office, Lusaka, 1973)
56. UN/ECA/FAO. Report of the Economic Survey Mission on the Economic Development of Zambia (Falcon Press, Ndola, 1964)
57. Williams, M. and C. Young, 'Social Cost Benefit Analysis and Zambia's Iron and Steel Project', Ministry of Finance and Ministry of Trade and Industry, April 1971 (mimeo).
58. Woakes, M.E., 'Iron "Ore-type" Occurrences in Zambia', MINDECO Ltd, 1972 (mimeo)

Other Sources

59. Banks, F.E., *The World Copper Market: An Economic Analysis* (Ballinger Publishing Co, Cambridge, Mass., 1974)
60. Banerjee, A.C. and M.B. Silgardo, 'The Economy of Size and Scale of Steelmaking Units with Particular Reference to the Indian Steel Industry', UNIDO/ID/WG. 146/79 (June 1973)
61. Barnes, R.S., '24th Hatfield Memorial Lecture: Eurosteelresearch', *Metals Technology* (March 1974)
62. Cartwright, W.F., 'Comparison of the Blast-Furnace/BOF Route with its Alternatives' in *Alternative Routes to Steel Making* (Iron and Steel Institute, London, 1971)
63. Chilton, C.H., '"Six-Tenths Factor" Applies to Complete Plant Costs' in C.H. Chilton (ed.), *Cost Engineering in the Process Industries* (McGraw-Hill, New York, 1960)

64.   Cockerill, A. and A. Silberston, *The Steel Industry: International Comparisons of Industrial Structure and Performance,* University of Cambridge, Department of Applied Economics, Occasional Paper No. 42 (C.U.P., Cambridge, 1974)

65.   Friden, L., *Instability in the International Steel Market* (Beckmans, Stockholm, 1972)

66.   IBRD. 'Price Forecasts of Major Primary Commodities', IBRD/IDA Report No. 467 (19 June 1974)

67.   Lawrence, Jr., R., 'The Hyl Direct Reduction Process: Past, Present and Future', UN/ECE/Steel Committee, May 1972.

68.   Marelle, A., 'The Iron Ore Market', UN/TAD/INT/SEM. 1/1, July 1970

69.   Miller, J.R., 'On-site Processing of Iron Ore in Developing Countries Through the Stage of Prereduced Agglomeration', UNIDO/ID/WG.146/67, May 1973.

70.   Milnor, J., 'Games Against Nature' in R.M. Thrall, C.H. Coombs and R.L. Davis (eds.), *Decision Processes* (John Wiley & Sons, New York, 1954)

71.   Mozer, I.A. and G.H. Laferriere, 'Midrex Reduction Plant: Part of Sidbec's Integrated Steelmaking', UNIDO/ID/WG.146/121, October 1973.

72.   *National Institute Economic Review,* No. 67 (February 1974)

73.   OECD. Annual Reports on the Iron and Steel Industry (Paris, 1964-1974)

74.   OECD. Main Economic Indicators, December 1970.

75.   OECD. Statistics of Foreign Trade: Monthly Bulletin, Series A, June 1974.

76.   Pratten, C., R.M. Dean, and A. Silberston, 'The Economies of Large Scale Production in British Industry', University of Cambridge, Department of Applied Economics, Occasional Paper No. 28, (C.U.P., Cambridge, 1971)

77.   UN/ECE. Comparison of Steel-making Processes (United Nations, New York, 1962)

78.   UN/ECE. World Trade in Steel and Steel Demand in Developing Countries (United Nations, New York, 1968)

79.   UNIDO. *Iron and Steel Industry,* UN/UNIDO/ID/40/5, 1969

80.   UNIDO Secretariat. *An Appraisal of Some of the Direct Reduction Processes for the Production of Sponge Iron,* UNIDO/ID/WG.146/118, September 1973

81.   Voice, E.W. and J.M. Ridgion, 'Changes in Ironmaking Technology in Relation to the Availability of Coking Coals', *Ironmaking and Steelmaking* (Quarterly), No. 7 (1974)

INDEX

For Product Safety Concerns and Information please contact our EU representative GPSR@taylorandfrancis.com Taylor & Francis Verlag GmbH, Kaufingerstraße 24, 80331 München, Germany

Printed and bound by CPI Group (UK) Ltd, Croydon, CR0 4YY
01/05/2025
01858411-0001